WHAT'S YOUR BIG THREE?

ABOUT THE AUTHOR

Andrea Taylor (Dorset, England) has been an astrological counselor for over forty years. Originally self-taught, she studied through the Huber School in the mid-1980s. She started teaching birth chart interpretation soon after, and she's had clients worldwide. Andrea also authored *The Astrology Book* and *Birth Chart Interpretation Plain & Simple*.

WHAT'S YOUR

BIG

THREE?

HOW *SUN, MOON &* *RISING* SIGNS REVEAL WHO YOU REALLY ARE

ANDREA TAYLOR

LLEWELLYN PUBLICATIONS | WOODBURY, MINNESOTA

FIRST EDITION
First Printing, 2022

Book design by Samantha Peterson
Cover design by Shira Atakpu

Llewellyn Publications is a registered trademark of Llewellyn Worldwide Ltd.

Library of Congress Cataloging-in-Publication Data (Pending)
ISBN: 978-0-7387-7061-1

Llewellyn Worldwide Ltd. does not participate in, endorse, or have any authority or responsibility concerning private business transactions between our authors and the public.

All mail addressed to the author is forwarded but the publisher cannot, unless specifically instructed by the author, give out an address or phone number.

Any internet references contained in this work are current at publication time, but the publisher cannot guarantee that a specific location will continue to be maintained. Please refer to the publisher's website for links to authors' websites and other sources.

Llewellyn Publications
A Division of Llewellyn Worldwide Ltd.
2143 Wooddale Drive
Woodbury, MN 55125-2989
www.llewellyn.com

Printed in the United States of America

OTHER BOOKS BY ANDREA TAYLOR

The Astrology Book
Birth Chart Interpretation Plain & Simple

CONTENTS

CHAPTER FOUR: SUN AND MOON SIGN COMBINATIONS — 169

INTRODUCTION

The birth chart is a diagrammatic photograph of the universe at that special moment we become part of it: when we draw our first breath. Like a map, it shows the energies we inherit, which in turn describe how we will act, how we love, how we think, what motivates us, and our fears and challenges. The positions of the sun and moon and the sign of our ascendant (otherwise known as the rising sign) at our moment of birth are the most important—and revealing—aspects of our personality.

It is easy to discover what your sun, moon, and rising sign are. Lots of computer sites can provide a picture of your birth chart and usually list the astrological signs the planets were in as well. To create an accurate birth chart you will be asked to enter the date, place, and time of birth. The latter is really important because the earth rotates as it orbits the sun, and at the same time the moon orbits the earth. As the chart is a picture of the sky at the moment of birth, the more accurate the time, the more accurate the chart.

However, even a vague birth time can lend a helping hand. For example, the sun stays in one sign for a long time (roughly a month), so unless you happen to be born on the day it changes signs, the day alone is enough to find that out. The moon stays in each sign two and a half days, so knowing the day is often enough. To be absolutely sure, read the descriptions of each sun or moon sign; if it doesn't sound like you, read the descriptions on either side to see if that is more accurate. The placement that is hard to determine without a time of birth is the rising sign, because that changes every two hours. Usually, the birth time is recorded on birth certificates, but older family members may also know.

If you haven't looked at your birth chart before, now is the time! Hop on a website (I recommend www.astrocalc .com on your computer or www.astro.com on your phone) to see what your chart looks like and where the planets are.

When you see your birth chart for the first time, you may be amazed at just how much there is in it. There are ten heavenly bodies/planets in our sky, all of which will appear on your chart, plus there are other symbols to reflect things like the north nodes—these indicate your karmic path—and aspect lines, those coloured lines that stretch across the middle of the chart and link planets. My book *Birth Chart Interpretation Plain & Simple* explains everything there is to know about understanding and interpreting your entire chart, so if you want to know more, I suggest ordering a copy.

THE IMPORTANCE OF SUN, MOON, AND RISING SIGNS

All the planets and symbols in a birth chart tell us something about who we are and how we act. Each planet has a purpose, an energy. For example, Mercury is the planet of communication. The astrological sign it is in shows how we communicate with others: if we are chatty or quiet, practical or academic. Venus shows how we love—whether we want a stable, secure partnership or prefer to have lighter, freer links with others. Mars shows what we want from life and where we direct our energy to achieve our life aims. So, why are the sun, moon, and rising sign the three most important aspects?

The sun is the most prominent planet in our sky. It keeps us alive with its warmth and light. In astrological terms it is our *will*; it is who we are. The sign it is in describes how we express our personality as a whole and is the basis from which all our actions emanate.

The moon is our emotional response to people and situations, and the astrological sign it is in shows how we *feel* about the things that happen to us, as well as what nurtures and comforts us. Most likely it will be in a completely different astrological sign than the sun (but not always). Already you can see how important the sun and moon are. They are the action energy (sun) and emotional energy (moon) that drive our lives.

The rising sign is not a planet. It is the *astrological sign* that is "rising" on the eastern horizon at the exact moment of birth. We use our rising sign as a filter when meeting people; we hide behind the qualities of this astrological sign when we first encounter others. It is our mask. Hiding behind our rising sign gives us time to decide whether we want to allow a new person to get to know us better. Therefore, it is what other people first feel/see when meeting us, and that is why it is so important.

THE SIGNS, THEIR ELEMENTS, AND THEIR MOTIVATIONS

Your sun and moon will occupy one of the twelve astrological signs, so before reading further it will be helpful to understand something about those signs. Throughout the book, references will be made to the sign's element. Each astrological sign is one of the four elements: fire, earth, air, or water. These elements describe how the signs act.

Aries, Leo, and Sagittarius are fire signs. Fire signs are action seekers, quick and impulsive. Earth signs seek security and stability, and their focus is on material gain. The earth signs are Taurus, Virgo, and Capricorn. Air signs use their minds; they are logical and a bit detached from emotional matters. Gemini, Libra, and Aquarius are air signs. Water signs base everything on how they feel. They are emotional, sensitive, and intuitive. The water signs are Cancer, Scorpio, and Pisces.

Each one of the signs also has a motivation. They are either cardinal, fixed, or mutable. Cardinal signs are proactive. If life pulls the rug out from under them, they can start again. The cardinal signs are Aries, Capricorn, Libra, and Cancer. Fixed signs do not like change and can be stubborn. The fixed signs are Leo, Taurus, Aquarius, and Scorpio. Mutable signs are flexible and adaptable. The mutable signs are Sagittarius, Virgo, Gemini, and Pisces.

Understanding the element and motivation of each sign is very revealing, so do take a moment to think about your own sun and moon signs. What are the elements and motivations of your sun and moon sign? How do these signs' elements and motivations affect the way you act and feel?

The positions of the sun, moon, and rising sign give us a very good idea of who someone is and of how they will act and react in most situations. So, sit back and enjoy reading about yourself and your loved ones (and perhaps your prospective partner, or your new boss). Knowledge is power, they say!

one
SUN SIGNS

Most people know about sun signs. Information is all around us; horoscopes are everywhere. But have you ever thought about why this one aspect has been chosen to represent the whole science of astrology?

We are a complex mix of many energies, but the bottom line is that we express our sun sign characteristics more fully than any other aspect of ourselves. It is our will, our life force, and everything we do is influenced by it. Our personality may be tempered by the positions of other planets but we are, first and foremost, our sun sign, and its influence weaves through every aspect of our lives.

The sun is the largest, brightest, and warmest planet in our solar system and keeps us alive—without its warmth,

Earth would be a barren, lifeless planet—so it is easy to see why ancient civilisations like the Mayans worshipped it. The astrological sign the sun is in when we are born describes our most obvious characteristics, traits we must outwardly express to be true to ourselves.

Our sun sign is determined by the astrological constellation the sun is in at our moment of birth. The sun is unique amongst the planets because, unlike the rest, it moves at almost exactly one degree a day, so we are able to assign calendar dates to it. We know where it will be at any given time.

The symbol for the sun is a round circle with a dot in the centre, so look at your chart and find where the sun is located. Do you recognise the astrological symbol on the part of the chart your sun is in? If not, find a list of astrological symbols to determine which sign your sun is in.

Each of the astrological signs has a purpose. Aries initiates, Taurus secures, Gemini passes on information, Cancer is the carer, Leo is the leader, Virgo attends to the details, Libra is the peacemaker, Scorpio is the in-depth researcher, Sagittarius is the truth seeker, Capricorn is the parent figure, Aquarius is the genius who discovers new things, and Pisces is the gentle old soul who has seen it all a thousand times before.

Each sign has positive and negative aspects, but these must be viewed in light of the sign's purpose. It is no good expecting Gemini to stay settled when its role is to move around delivering messages, just as expecting Aries to be able to attend to details is impossible when they are meant to start projects, not to stay around to finish them. Virgo loves that job, but they would hate to be responsible for beginning something. So, each sign has its role.

That is why a knowledge of astrology is so vital, especially when hiring people for jobs or looking for a relationship. We won't expect the impossible from someone once we understand their life role, and it can save a lot of money in business and a great deal of emotional hassle if we enter into relationships with people knowing their true nature.

Use astrology as a tool for self-understanding, but also apply it to those you know and love. Allowing others to be themselves and not what we wish them to be is the key to happiness and understanding in our friendships and relationships.

Now go have some fun discovering new things about yourself, your friends, your partner, and your family!

♈
SUN IN ARIES

Motivation and Element: Cardinal fire

Symbol: The ram

Ruled by: Mars

Sun Sign Dates: March 21 to April 19

Positive Traits: Happy, chatty, friendly, active, upbeat, optimistic, able to quickly recover from disasters

Negatives: Argumentative, a bit bossy, wants their own way, insensitive to the needs of others

Aries have an irrepressibly buoyant nature. Their cheerful, direct good humour is a breath of fresh air. When they appear on the scene, people know things will get done. Sitting in meetings is anathema to them—all that talk, talk, talk bores them rigid. They are action people. Being ruled by the warlike planet Mars gives them energy and drive, so they are not going to be sitting around waiting for things to happen—they are going to be the one making it happen.

Aries has a double dose of energy. Aries is a fire sign, so they are impetuous and impulsive, but it's also a cardinal sign, meaning they are proactive, so they like a target, a challenge, and activity. All this fire energy means they are fast off the mark in everything they do. Aries' enthusiasm is quickly alight, and without much prior thought they leap in and start projects. Being so optimistic, they are confident everything will work out fine. When it doesn't, no one is more surprised than Aries, but nothing fazes them—not for long, anyway. They adore being challenged in life, and they are always at their best when the gauntlet is thrown down.

Aries is the first sign of the zodiac and their manner is likened to a child: yesterday didn't exist and tomorrow is too far away; it is today that matters. Everything is immediate and personal. When they speak, it's always about them: "I want," "I like," "I need." This is not intentionally selfish. This first sign is all about "me," which is why Aries always thinks of themselves first and others afterward. This is how it is supposed to be!

Like a child, they are full of warm, bright enthusiasm, and they blindly trust in fate. Yet, they rarely need a shoulder to cry on if things don't work out because they are incredibly resilient. Coming up with a new plan is their way of fighting the doldrums—not that they are ever down for long. Aries are not people for whom depression, despair, or despondency ever takes root, except for the briefest moment, soon to be replaced by enthusiasm for another challenge. Time and time again, despite disasters of every kind—physical, mental, and emotional—Aries pick themselves up and start all over again. Their personal courage is extraordinary. A new idea soon occurs, and this time it will work, they are sure. Aries is probably the one sign that takes a little longer to learn from mistakes.

Because Aries's needs always come first, they are often brusque when people ask for too much of their time. Fitting in with others—compromising—is impossible for Aries unless they have some softer elements in their chart. That is why they are often accused of insensitivity. And yes, they can be insensitive, but others rarely take umbrage because they know it doesn't stem from deliberate unkindness, but rather from that single-minded forward movement so necessary to the sign of Aries.

Too busy being busy to be interested in controlling others, Aries are incredibly naive, trusting, and gullible, which leaves them vulnerable to those who are manipulative. Seeing only the best in people and being so straight and honest, they are often deceived or misled by others, both in business and in romance.

Being a warm, confident sign, they are never short of partners. It is *maintaining* relationships Aries find hard because they really dislike overly emotional behaviour; being around people who moan, criticise, or are depressed brings them down. They don't have the tools to help needy people because their motto is to focus on something new, so if others don't take their advice and dry their eyes, Aries leaves. They'll find something else to do!

They detest people giving them advice, especially warnings of danger ahead. Aries never heed wise words. It only frustrates and irritates them when people offer suggestions. Without some softer aspects in their chart, Aries can be impatient, argumentative, aggressive, and confrontational. Because Aries is ruled by Mars, if they are stopped from going down a route they want to take, they are quite capable of getting annoyed and expressing that anger. Their symbol is the ram, who attacks life by battering through obstacles, and that is always their approach.

Their friendly, upbeat manner is what people love most about them. Aries are action-oriented people who inspire others with their cheerful optimism that tomorrow will be a brighter day.

QUICK SUMMARY OF ARIES

Impulsive, intuitive, friendly, chatty, active, outgoing. Aries enjoy challenges, like being busy. Often tomboys. Sporty, trusting, gullible, naive, optimistic. Always sees the bright side; enthusiastic and energetic. Impetuous, bossy, and outspoken. Hardheaded and impatient, unable to compromise in relationships, and must have their own way. The subtle arts of seduction and romance are too slow and boring for them. Not empathic or emotional—crybabies irritate them. They act quickly in everything they do, usually before thinking or planning. Good at setting things in motion but not so good at following up. Can let go and move on when things don't work in relationships and projects. Tough and courageous. Can be aggressive and confrontational if there aren't softer planets in their charts. Astrological purpose is to initiate things.

♉
SUN IN TAURUS

Motivation and Element: Fixed earth

Symbol: The bull

Ruled by: Venus

Sun Sign Dates: April 20 to May 20

Positive Traits: Reliable, trustworthy, stable, calm, family-minded, good cook

Negatives: Implacable and stubborn, lacks an adventurous spirit

Renowned for great patience, huge amounts of endurance, and incredible tolerance, Taurus has broad shoulders. They are a bit slow to act, resistant to change, and not likely to set the world on fire, but in our fast-changing world it is wonderful to find people who manage to ride the ups and downs of life with calm equanimity and stay just as they have always been: unruffled, unfazed, and unaffected by fads and fashions. Taureans enshrine the old-fashioned values of our forefathers, and they are as solid as a rock.

Say hello to Taurus, the bull, the fixed earth sign who is exactly what it says on the tin. If they say they will help, they will. If they promise to meet, they will be there. If others need help, they capably assist them in practical ways. Taurus can earn money, build a house, decorate it, dig the garden, look after babies with amazing patience, prepare a delicious meal, and still look as if they haven't a care in the world. They manage life; a feat the rest of us can only be in awe of. Whatever life throws at them, they cope, survive, and thrive.

Taureans don't overreact, get emotional, cry and scream, or get so drunk they end up in the gutter at three in the morning (though they like a drink, but they can usually handle it). Nor will they be marching with banners for some obscure or not-so-obscure cause. Their attention is fully occupied by creating security for themselves and their family. With incredible strength and patience, they steadily build, wrapping loved ones in comfort and safety.

Is there a downside? Well, of course there is. It is unlikely Taurus will be bungee jumping off the Eiffel Tower, abseiling down the Empire State Building, or any other unproductive (and expensive) stunt. Taurus likes their feet firmly planted on the ground in every respect, literally and figuratively.

Taureans view change with distrust, if not outright fear. If something has always worked, why alter it? When things stay the same, they feel safe, and they don't like the ground moving beneath their feet.

And if this sign says no, people might as well save their time trying to change Taurus's mind. Fixed signs never change their minds. So, they are stubborn as well as unadventurous. And partners might find their love and care a bit claustrophobic sometimes, because Taurus tends toward possessiveness. Nor are they going to astound with their clever ideas or innovative designs; to be honest, they are usually monosyllabic. Why waste words? Why waste anything for no return? All effort is extended for a purpose, and that is to build. Long conversations are meaningless for Taurus, unless it is a practical discussion on how to make sure the woodshed is kept dry.

So, Taurus won't do lots of things others would like to have a go at, but on the other hand nothing delights them more than being outside. They love nature because Taurus is an earth sign, so the outdoors is their natural habitat. The sounds and smells of nature appeal to their senses: the smell of flowers, gazing up at an azure sky with the autumn leaves crunching underfoot, woodsmoke from a campfire, bacon cooking on a stove, a wild ocean crashing against rocks, swimming naked then sleeping on the beach, watching the sun rise and walking hand in hand through the dunes with a loved one… These are the things that get Taurus up at the crack of dawn or out for the night—anything that stimulates their five senses. Partying in stuffy, noisy bars is not one of them.

The sixth sense, the spiritual side of life, will be of little interest. It is the solid and tangible Taurus likes, the things they can use and touch and make. It takes enough of their energy to live in the here and now; they certainly don't extend any thought to what comes next or why we are here in the first place. Fact: we are here. Fact: one day we will die. Wondering about something that is impossible to answer is a meaningless waste of time and energy.

Sensuous and loving yet implacable, Taurus tolerates an enormous amount from others. They stand back and watch others rushing here and there, getting stressed for no reason and for no reward, and shake their head. Yet, when life falls apart for someone, Taurus always steps forward. Their love and friendship is forever, and they don't give up or walk away just because things got tough or people lost their way. Taurus was made for tough. In an unstable and ever-changing world, it is reassuring and comforting that one thing will never change: Taurus.

QUICK SUMMARY OF TAURUS

Stick-in-the-mud, traditional, family-minded. Seeks stability and is possessive of belongings and people they perceive as theirs. Slow to change and slow to anger, but once roused capable of great outrage. Reliable, dependable, and practical, but rarely introspective, and never intuitive. Earthy appetites, with a love of food and drink and an inability to deny themselves sensual pleasures, which means they are rarely slim. Money and belongings are important. Hard-working and very stubborn. Implacable and unmoveable once they have decided on something. People of few words.

Often resides in same house all their life. Seeks partners who will build alongside them. Their love is given forever, so they find it hard to let go of people.

♊
SUN IN GEMINI

Motivation and Element: Mutable air

Symbol: The twins

Ruled by: Mercury

Sun Sign Dates: May 21 to June 20

Positive Traits: Light, airy, talkative, friendly, live-and-let-live attitude, great with words

Negatives: Unreliable, insensitive to the needs of others, avoids commitment

Gemini is an air sign, so they want their life to be a lighthearted affair, with humour and friendship being the most important aspects. Words are their forte, so whether it is chatting, teaching others, writing or giving talks, being on television or in the movies, or working with information technology, any and all forms of communication are areas in which Geminis excel.

As a mutable sign, they are adaptable and flexible. They can easily change their opinions in discussions, often agreeing with whomever they are talking to. This acceptance draws others out, which provides more information.

Their astrological job is to pass on information, so the more they can get people to talk, the more information they can collect, and the more they can pass on to the next person. This flexible approach is deliberate; Geminis are not meant to be tied to one place or one person, but others constantly misunderstand and accuse Gemini of being unreliable. Yes, they are, but they are meant to be. Not everyone can be (or should be) grounded and stable; let's leave that to the earth signs.

When it comes to relationships, obviously this can cause a few issues. Most partners expect some sort of emotional and financial support, neither of which Gemini gives much thought to. They like to keep things cool and friendly, so they seek someone they can talk to. The physical side is fine, and Geminis are only human, but it is people's thoughts and ideas that really float their boat. First and foremost they seek friendship with their partner, and everything else will follow from there. As for finances, Gemini will probably earn more than enough to live comfortably because they simply must be out in the world, living a busy, active, interesting life. But it won't be deliberate or thought-out; like many things in Gemini's life, it will just happen.

Unlike earth signs, Geminis are not driven by ambition or security, but they need to be right at the forefront of change, be it cultural, intellectual, medical, technical, scientific, or artistic. The giver of messages cannot pass on information without knowing the very latest, so they naturally gravitate to where things are happening so they can be in the know. That's why Geminis are so prevalent in all the above-mentioned professions, using their words: talking, gossiping, speaking, writing, passing on information. Even with a more ordinary career, they still seek the latest information and act as a messenger, but in the community rather than on a global stage. All of it is important.

It is a well-documented fact that Geminis often have two of everything; their symbol is the twins. But in reality, we all have a dual nature: when we are feeling our best and when we aren't. With Gemini, the lovely, friendly twin is replaced by the caustic, snappy, critical twin when they feel trapped, down, or unwell. Any unkindness will come in the form of words. But that is it, and it won't last long because Geminis are naturally buoyant people who enjoy being light and fun, so they never wallow in prolonged self-pity.

And yes, because of their flexible, airy nature, variety is important to Gemini. When things get stale and predictable, they feel the urge to move on. Many Geminis do have more than one long-term partner during their lives. Children are a delight, but they relate better to teenagers, when they can really talk and share activities. The early years of parenthood are difficult for someone who needs to be on the move, and the constant crying and constraints are not bearable for long. Thus, Geminis often unconsciously choose a caring partner who might enjoy that aspect.

The past is of no interest to a true Gemini because it is of no use to their astrological job. More likely, they will be reading the latest books, scanning the most up-to-date magazines, gathering information about the newest scientific or medical breakthrough, picking up gossip about celebrities and film stars, finding the best places to go, and learning about trendy hairstyles, makeup, and clothing. This is their job, and Gemini should remind people of that when others accuse them of being unreliable!

QUICK SUMMARY OF GEMINI

Enjoys any new form of communication. Likes being in the know, up-to-date, and where it's at. Picks up information at surface level, so able to lightly discuss many subjects but rarely in depth. Changeable and restless, flexible and fun. Uses words cleverly and will choose a career that reflects that. Loves telling jokes and uses them to lighten the mood. Symbol is the twins, so they have two sides to their personality and can switch between each at the drop of a hat. Hard to pin down in word or deed. Never puts anything in writing because they might not think tomorrow the way they do today. Not good at long-term commitments because of their need for variety and change. Friendly and light. Enjoys conversation with partners.

Cannot cope with people who are emotional, dramatic, or dependent, and makes a quick exit. Always fashionable. Knows the latest gossip. The messenger of the zodiac.

♋
SUN IN CANCER

Motivation and Element: Cardinal water

Symbol: The crab

Ruled by: The moon

Sun Sign Dates: June 21 to July 22

Positive Traits: Caring, sympathetic, sentimental, empathic, emotionally receptive, loving

Negatives: Overly emotional, self-pitying, overprotective

The sign of Cancer is renowned for being the most emotional of the water signs. Although there are three water signs, the other two have very different approaches because Scorpio is fixed (stubborn and determined) while Pisces is mutable (changeable and hard to pin down). Cancer, on the other hand, is cardinal, and this makes them not only inwardly sensitive, but outwardly capable and strong.

Most of the caring professions have a liberal sprinkling of Cancer souls who actively go out of their way to help alleviate suffering—probably because they know exactly how painful everything is. Empathy and understanding are their number one lovely traits, along with compassion for everyone who suffers. Atrocities bring them to tears, and if they see someone immediately in need of aid, they rush to do what they can; never in a million years would Cancer walk on by pretending it is nothing to do with them.

And this is why they get so upset when people are unkind toward them or their family. Being so easily hurt, Cancer's tender feelings are always being trodden on. There are an awful lot of unfeeling people out there, saying and doing things without thought of the consequences. This sign, out of all the others, is the one who feels it most. A misplaced word, an imagined insult (if they are feeling tired or stressed), or an outright attack, and their first thought is to dash home, aggrieved and weepy. At those moments it is hard not to recall all the previous times life has dealt them a similar blow, and Cancer wonders why people cannot just be kind and pleasant and help each other.

Cancer's symbol is the crab. This epitomises Cancer's vulnerability without its shell. Those cruel verbal barbs go straight to their tender underbelly. When they do so much for people, it's very hard to handle someone being unkind. They are the one sign that can go from happy to sad in the blink of an eye, and this mood shift is often so fast and unpredictable it is hard to judge why. Being ultrasensitive makes them highly intuitive to atmospheres as well, so words are not always needed to upset them.

Once Cancer has had time to recover and dry their eyes, they climb back into their shell and head out into the world again. They do this courageous thing despite their pain because Cancer's top priority is building emotional security. Finding that special someone who will be supportive and caring when they are hurt is paramount. They simply could not bear an insensitive partner who told them to get on with it. They need cuddles and encouraging words, someone who understands why they are so upset and who makes them feel deeply loved and appreciated. Fortunately, most Cancerians end up with just the sort of partner they need.

If there are children—most Cancerians are afraid they will not make good enough parents, so they usually wait a bit longer before having them—they will suffer a thousand pains for them, too. Cancer parents endeavour to protect their children from each and every hurt of life, but of course it isn't possible, so they give them what they themselves most need: love and support.

Cancerians are nostalgic and sentimental, so the past is as dear to them as the present. People they have loved and lost are often recalled, be it lovers, friends, or family. Most Cancerians like nothing more than leafing through old letters, emails, photos, or their hoard of stashed memories.

All signs have failings, and Cancer's is a tendency to smother loved ones. It's a fine line between genuine support and overprotectiveness. This will only be obvious to their children when they're old enough to fly the nest, and they may go quicker than Cancer would like. And Cancer's temperamental natures make them hard work sometimes, with their loved ones always trying to avoid treading on their ultrasensitive toes.

Devoted, deeply caring, nurturing, and totally loyal, Cancer is the most loving sign in a truly hands-on way, and they give profound love to those they care about.

QUICK SUMMARY OF CANCER

Emotional, sometimes overly so. Protective of themselves and loved ones. Sentimental, views the past through rose-coloured spectacles. Emotionally vulnerable and easily hurt. Cries a lot, tends to feel sorry for themselves, temperamental, finds it hard to let go of the memory of a rejection or of people who have once been important to them. Driven to create emotional security. Seeks partners who are compassionate and understanding and can give Cancer a hug when hurt. Thinks that showing emotional support to others is important. Enjoys the nurturing side of life and anything that shows they care, such as food, warmth, comfort, and cuddles. Long talks about emotions are important to them. Best jobs are those that look after others: doctor, nurse, carer, cook, paramedic, etc. Can be over-possessive and overprotective of loved ones. Holds grudges when they've been hurt.

♌
SUN IN LEO

Motivation and Element: Fixed fire

Symbol: The lion

Ruled by: The sun

Sun Sign Dates: July 23 to August 22

Positive Traits: Charismatic, charming, natural leader, warm, loving, protective

Negatives: Proud, conceited, arrogant, bossy, needs constant praise

Leo's symbol is the lion, the king of the jungle, so there will be a certain something about them that sets them apart from everyone else. It could be that charismatic glow in their eyes or the confident, assured manner Leos have—whatever it is, people sense their leadership qualities and defer to them. That is why many Leos are in high positions. They are captains of ships, army generals, and heads of prestigious organisations. They are charity presidents giving keynote speeches at conferences. They are the actors who hold an audience in the palm of their hands; this is Leo at its best.

Leo needs a stage on which to shine, and even if it is only their own family who allow them that spotlight, it is important for them to be number one in the hearts of those they know. Being ruled by the sun, Leo simply must be able to express themselves, and that inner warmth and energy is the powerhouse from which their courageous heart derives all of its purpose. Given the right amount of appreciation, their warmth and love are like the sun itself: all-encompassing.

They are capable of the greatest of sacrifices, and they will rush in without thought when someone weaker or in danger needs help. Like the lion, Leo keeps loved ones from harm, and they use this strength in every aspect of their life. They enjoy nothing more than organising a fundraising event for a worthy cause. Leo prefers not to dirty their hands with menial work, and with their charm, elegance, and persuasive manner, it's easy for them to get others to do those things.

Being a fire sign, Leo is warm and impulsive, brave and fearless. They fully enter into life, and they give their all when required. The classic job for a Leo is an actor, but when the chips are down, they can always pursue business; all the high-profile roles in an organisation are about publicity, advertising, and being seen and heard. Leos thrive in the public eye; the grander the event, the better. But, like an actor, Leo needs praise for a job well done.

This is their stumbling block: their need for appreciation. Despite having more charisma than any of the other signs, despite being commanding and courageous, they need to hear people clapping. They really need to hear "Thank you"—or better yet, someone saying Leo is absolutely the best they have ever known. Admiration pushes Leo even further. There is nothing Leo won't do for a person once they simply acknowledge their superior status.

There are some apparently modest Leos. Don't be misled. While on the surface they may appear modest (and this depends on their rising sign), deep inside they have this same need to be the centre of attention, even if it is only within their family. They want to be the hub around which everything revolves, and Leos adore nothing more than attentive family who really appreciate all the sacrifices they have made—and continue to make—to keep everyone safe from harm. In return, Leos expect never to be ignored, forgotten, or abandoned. And like that lion, if anyone dares attack those they love, they take no prisoners.

Has this paragon of charm any faults? Of course! Their commanding manner sometimes comes across as bossiness. Leo likes to be in charge, and even though some manage this feat without sounding bossy, they always have to be number one in any setting. They rarely make friends with someone who might usurp their position. And when Leo does a good job and gets that praise, it can make them a little conceited. They may well have reason to be, but other people don't like someone who is so obviously proud of themselves.

It can be hard, too, for others to keep up the constant praise that is so necessary for Leo's self-esteem. Yet, with their stubborn streak—Leo is a fixed sign and all fixed signs are stubborn—they will never admit to any mistakes or apologise. Something inside Leo dies if they have to say sorry. Rather than do so, they will walk away with head held high. If others back down, Leo will immediately forgive them, but they find it impossible to apologise because that is an admission of being incorrect, and people simply cannot expect the sun to be at fault!

Leo is at their very best on the stage of life. They adore dressing up and going out or, even better, going where the rich and famous hang out. Looking good is important, and Leo will take any number of pains (and spend as much as they have to) in order to make sure they look suitably glamorous for any occasion. Overspending is the norm. They choose partners who also look the part, because appearances are important since Leo wants to hang out at the best places with the top people. Even the quieter Leos love dressing up, partying, driving expensive cars, and going to the best places.

It is important for Leo to love, to be loved, and to stand out from the crowd. The grander the life, the happier they will be. They want their life to be a colourful, dramatic performance met with loud applause. Take a bow, Leo.

QUICK SUMMARY OF LEO

The lion accurately describes their innate dignity and pride. Demands (and requires) respect. Warm, loving, and protective. Like the lion, enjoys strutting their stuff and being admired by family and friends. Prefers positions of authority. Never feels happy in a lowly position in life. Doesn't have to be in the limelight—though many actors/television personalities have an important planet in Leo—but needs a position where their talents are recognised. Praise is essential and encourages them to be even better. Vain, generous, and affectionate, but can roar in anger if annoyed. If there is too strong an emphasis on Leo in a chart, it can show itself as weakness to flattery, a need for constant praise, and conceit. Likes to be noticed when they enter a room. Somehow manages to get others to do the menial work.

♍
SUN IN VIRGO

Motivation and Element: Mutable earth

Symbol: The earth maiden

Ruled by: Mercury

Sun Sign Dates: August 23 to September 22

Positive Traits: Dutiful, kind, helpful, earthy, hardworking, sexy

Negatives: Fussy, nitpicky, a worrier

Virgo is the earth maiden who attends to the practical duties of life, so their focus is on service to others.
Their lives are often about doing things that help the rest
of us. That may sound dull to some, but they experience
an inner satisfaction when they are helpful. Virgos serve
others who need care, make sure every task gets done,
and neatly tidy up the messes other people leave behind.
Being modest and dutiful, Virgo prefers to work behind
the scenes, happily leaving limelight to the others.

Details; it is all about details for Virgo. With Mercury
as their ruler, they are incredibly smart and clever with
words. They have a great sense of wry humour, which is
often directed at the failings of others. It is hard not to be
critical when they see things so clearly! When they meet
someone new, Virgo instinctively takes in everything
about them: their clothes, hairstyle, manners, accent, and
mannerisms. Critical, certainly, and hard to please, but they
make astute judgments, too, and they are invariably right
in their first impressions. It is easy to make light of Virgo's
attention to details but, in truth, it is both a blessing and
a curse.

In every walk of life, details and organisation are key
to things running smoothly and safely. There are Virgos

everywhere: kind, earthy, sensible people going about making sure the rest of us live calm, safe lives, blithely unaware that Virgos are beavering away behind the scenes. Hardworking and practical, they organise everything so that life runs like clockwork. They are not showy or demanding. They don't need praise or wallow in self-pity, and they don't want to set the world on fire; they just want to be of help. But they are hard taskmasters—both of themselves and of others—because they expect perfection at home and at work. It's easy to spot a house where a Virgo lives. They usually adopt a minimalist style, and their home will most definitely be spotless. Being so industrious and painstaking in everything they do, it's hard for others to live up to Virgo's high standards and expectations, so their partners need a relaxed attitude toward their constant desire for perfection.

The reality is that the world is a disorganised place, and people are less than perfect, so Virgo has a never-ending job trying to bring order out of chaos. They create lists of jobs to do and then stay awake at night thinking about them. They worry they won't manage to get everything done on time. Sometimes it can all get to be too much. Sometimes they feel completely overfaced by the enormity of a task. Why can't the family just do a few of the small jobs so that they don't have to? Why can't everyone be a bit tidier and leave less work for them? Virgo sees mess everywhere: the house, the car, the garden, the office, the world. Now and then, understandably, this overload leads to a tendency to fret and nag.

The truth is, no one does a better job than Virgo. Others don't even see all the faults and failings in their environment—the wonky picture, the scratch on the car, the biscuit crumbs on the sofa—but Virgo's laser eye spots it all.

This need for order and neatness extends to their own body image. Virgos like to dress modestly because they don't want to stand out, but their clothes will be spotless and perfectly designed for the job at hand. They enjoy healthy food, and they are fussy about their intake. Most of them follow some sort of eating regime, be it vegetarian, vegan, or just straightforward healthy and organic. Exercise will be important too. Getting out and away from work is essential for their well-being, so going for a jog, a cycle ride, or a hike not only keeps them fit, it clears their head. Virgo is a mutable earth sign, which means they are flexible and adaptable, but they do have strict rules for themselves. Self-discipline could be every Virgo's middle name, so they have no problem sticking to whatever food regime they are following and whatever exercise plan they have devised in detail. The real problem will be stopping them from becoming obsessed with it!

Virgos dislike expressing their inner feelings until they know someone well. Being innately modest means they are reserved. Virgos are so modest, in fact, that when someone asks them out on a date, they may wonder if the person meant it or was just being kind. Underneath that eye for detail is a very earthy, sexy person just looking for a mate to give their all to. All Virgos are passionate in the bedroom—best, though, that partners dim the lights so Virgo can't get distracted by the jobs that need doing!

QUICK SUMMARY OF VIRGO

Practical, service-minded, dutiful, enjoys attention to detail. Works best behind the scenes, out of the limelight, doing what they do best—organisation and planning. Any and all detailed work appeals, whether that means creating a filing system, solving unsolved crimes, working as a personal assistant, balancing accounts, train and bus timetabling, editing, designing, or engineering. Enjoys serving others. Feels especially good when finding a mistake that others have missed. No need for praise. Serves selflessly and can deny themselves pleasures to attend to duties. Gives a day's work for a day's pay and never shirks their responsibilities. Worst fault is being critical of others and seeing glaring faults that no one else notices; thus, they can become fussy naggers. Sometimes needs to be dragged away from work because they always have a to-do list. Can't abide uncleanliness in person or place. Sexy.

⏜

SUN IN LIBRA

Motivation and Element: Cardinal air

Symbol: The scales

Ruled by: Venus

Sun Sign Dates: September 23 to October 22

Positive Traits: Balanced, logical, calm, reasonable, attractive, harmony-seeking

Negatives: Cool, detached, lazy at times, snobbish

A sign ruled by Venus itself is bound to be special, and it cannot be denied most Libras are beautiful (or at the very least, attractive) with oodles of charm and a cool, calm elegance. Libras usually have a dimple or two and somehow manage to look good even at their worst. With a flash of a smile or a twinkle of their alluring eye, Libra can persuade anyone to do almost anything. They will use that ability to the fullest, enabling their life to be the peaceful, luxurious, harmonious haven they dream of, as far removed from the rougher elements of life as humanly possible.

Libra is often accused of being a bit snobbish, but in reality it is fear that inspires their desire for the very best. It's impossible for them to work from a base that is crude, harsh, or unpleasant, or to live in a place where there are noisy, rowdy, aggressive people. It upsets their inner balance, which is hard enough to maintain at the best of times. Libra seeks to make their own life peaceful, calm, and beautiful, and only then can they go on to fulfil their astrological purpose—to bring harmony and balance to other people's lives.

That is why Libra's symbol is the scales. But those scales are hard to keep level, and they will dip up and down regularly. When the scales are in balance, Libra is at their very best; leaping out of bed at dawn to go for a run is not a problem. But when the scales dip, Libra feels drained of energy and won't get off the sofa all day. That is why their sign is sometimes called lazy. They are, but only half the time.

Libra rules partnerships, so it is important for them to have one, but they approach partnership as they approach everything else: with a cool logic. Oddly, despite being ruled by the planet of love (Venus), Libras are emotionally reserved and not renowned for their passion. They always make logical decisions, even in love, and are never swayed by anything except someone's appearance and bank account. Libra always looks good and wants to be seen with someone equally lovely. Their interest in someone's bank balance is not necessarily mercenary because with their powerful intellect, most Libras are capable of creating their own luxurious style of living, but it is important that prospective mates meet their standards or surpass them in every respect. Everything they do is with the aim of removing themselves from the grittier side of life. So, in reality, Libra reacts to circumstances rather than feelings when it comes to selecting a life partner. Their head always rules their heart.

With their clever logic and way with words, Libras make great lawyers, but they are good in any job that brings people together. They also excel at design and planning. Libra's ideal job would be one in which they are given lots of money to plan an event. With their natural eye for beauty, they always know classy from shoddy; they're very discerning. They also make great facilitators and mediators and are fabulous at public relations. Wherever Libra finds themselves, their aim is beauty, fairness, and justice.

Most Libras have help with the more mundane aspects of life. Scrubbing the floors, cleaning out the oven, weeding the garden, or putting out the garbage are not areas Venus likes to go. And if children come along, they will be dressed nicely, taught how to behave, and encouraged to play quietly with their siblings. There will be a nanny or, at the very least, willing older family members for frequent childcare so Libra can head out to have a drink and a meal somewhere classy.

Being a cardinal sign, Libra has the drive and energy to make the life they really want, and when circumstances change and the rug is pulled out from under them, they are more than capable of picking themselves up and starting again. Their aim will always be a peaceful existence surrounded by nice people. Libra will expend any amount of energy to create a calm lifestyle because until they have that, they cannot focus on anything else; Venus thrives in a gentle atmosphere.

Life is often gritty, though, and people can be aggressive. Libra tends to lie awake at night trying to find a solution to a problem. It sounds easy just being nice, calm, and reasonable, but Libras know all too well that it takes a great deal of energy to try to please everyone all of the time. But if anyone can do it, Libra can.

QUICK SUMMARY OF LIBRA

Balanced, sensible, reasonable, logical, harmony-seeking—just as you would expect from someone with the scales as their symbol. Not always in balance, though; can swing to extremes throughout their lives. Best traits: keeps the peace and rarely loses their temper or raises their voice. Sees both sides to an argument and is able to justify both. Seeks justice and fairness. Worst trait: lazy. Capable of doing nothing for weeks on end while jobs pile up. Also, annoying as a partner because of their inability to get off the fence and support loved ones when the need arises. Has a quiet, pleasing voice and never looks unkempt, even at their worst. Unfailingly polite. Stays calm in the midst of turmoil. Cool in relationships. Seeks to be removed from anything unpleasant, so prefers a partner who is rich. Clever, so can also make their own way.

♏

SUN IN SCORPIO

Motivation and Element: Fixed water

Symbol: The scorpion

Ruled by: Pluto

Sun Sign Dates: October 23 to November 21

Positive Traits: Passionate, intense, driven, ambitious, loyal, protective

Negatives: Jealous, possessive, suspicious, vengeful

The famed sign of Scorpio: passionate and intense, jealous and possessive, deep and unfathomable. If you've ever met a Scorpio, you may be thinking, *Surely not?* That is what most people think when they meet one. So incredibly good is Scorpio's disguise, it fools most people. They look as if nothing bothers them and as if they haven't a care in the world—but that couldn't be further from the truth. Just reading this will please a Scorpio because that is their aim: disguise.

Scorpios have to disguise their feelings behind this calm facade because they are so strong and deep and passionate that they might alarm others. And this is not just when it comes to close relationships—everything Scorpio undertakes is approached with a focused intensity of purpose. Whether a job, hobby, skill, or person, Scorpios invest the same amount of commitment and drive, the same level of passionate curiosity. They want to get to the very bottom of things; the superficial is not for them. That is why they make good researchers, engineers, detectives, scientists, and physicists. They excel in any career that involves problem-solving because Scorpios need to be stretched and tested. They enjoy pushing themselves to their limits. Otherwise, they feel that life is too easy, and easy is of no interest.

Scorpio is a fixed water sign. That means they are emotional and base decisions on their intuition, and Scorpio's intuition is second to none. They can home in on weak spots, which is why they are clever enough to find elusive answers to difficult problems; they can spot the way through, the path no one else has taken, the one everyone missed. It is not that they think outside of the box, like Aquarius. Rather, they see the overview. Nothing slips past their radar. Scorpios use this gift in all areas of life, so they are able to offer solutions for any situation, from an engineering problem to breakthroughs in research.

Solving a problem that appears insolvable is something a true Scorpio simply cannot resist, both because of the challenge to their intellect and because it gives them a chance to show their abilities and have their talents recognised. Scorpio's inner sense of self-worth is so strong that not for a single moment do they consider failure as an option.

Being a fixed sign means they are incredibly stubborn and believe they are always right—or, rather, they *know* they are always right. Nothing about Scorpio is wishy-washy, and their inner certainty is as fixed as everything else.

Because of this canny cleverness, it's not hard for them to quickly rise to the top of a profession. Answering to someone else is like dying a tiny bit inside. And when they do get an accolade or promotion, no one will know from their expression how much it means—even though it means everything—because not a flicker of emotion will flit across their face. Their eyes might shine a little brighter, to be sure, but unless people are very astute, they won't have the tiniest inkling how meaningful recognition is. Scorpio always knows they are the best, so it's important that others realise it as well.

Deep passion and intense feelings always give rise to negatives, which is why Scorpios are famed for their jealousy and possessiveness. This is not a myth. Their inner feelings are so intense that they take nothing lightly, and if they are suspicious others are not being completely honest and open with them, they will do whatever it takes to find out the truth. If someone they trusted betrays them, their cold anger has no bounds. It will simply be a matter of how evolved Scorpio is as to whether they take some form of active revenge or immediately cut that person out of their life as if they no longer exist.

Entering into a relationship with a Scorpio will be a full-time job. They are so intent on extremes, of experiencing everything to its limit, that it takes a sturdy heart and a strong constitution to survive their constant suspiciousness. Most gentle signs run for cover once they realise what they are up against, but there will be others who will rise to the challenge, and my goodness, Scorpio just loves that. It is like a gauntlet thrown down. Although they love deeply and are loyal and passionate, it is the challenges of life that excite them most. When someone accepts the challenge, they give a wide, apparently innocent smile, all the while thinking, *Let the games begin.*

QUICK SUMMARY OF SCORPIO

Best word to describe Scorpio is passion; that goes for everything they do. No action or thought is lighthearted. Likes to delve to the depths of anything that interests them, be it a person or a job or a hobby. Capable of deep emotion. Likes to analyse people to find out what makes them tick. Secretive, intense, driven, and manipulative—especially if they can benefit. Must have total control at work or in a relationship but can bide their time, sublimating their own desires to get what they want, and when they have it, woe betide anyone who attempts to take it away. Fierce and compelling when the chips are down. Scarily furious and capable of taking revenge. Not the person to play games with. Their coldness is more dangerous than their passion.

♐
SUN IN SAGITTARIUS

Motivation and Element: Mutable fire

Symbol: The archer

Ruled by: Jupiter

Sun Sign Dates: November 22 to December 21

Positive Traits: Exciting, friendly, fun, sociable, energetic, optimistic

Negatives: Unreliable, avoids commitments, blunt

The symbol of Sagittarius is the archer, who fires his arrows into the air, one after the other. This accurately sums up Sagittarius's scattered energy and need to have many irons in the fire. Just when they have finished one adventure, they are off on another: following another idea or studying something different. Sagittarians can keep half a dozen things on the go at once and easily juggle them all. That's how they like it, because then boredom will never set in. They move effortlessly from one project to another as the mood takes them, sometimes finishing things, some-times not—all the while making multitasking look like a walk in the park.

Being so busy and active, it is easy to lose track of them-selves. Their impulsive, fiery, active, adventurous nature impels them ever onward. For Sagittarius, life is all about experiences and adventures, lots of them, all of which teach them something, all of which add to their personal philosophy. They never refuse an invitation because they are afraid of missing something.

Being a mutable fire sign, their life force could be described as *moving action*. It is all about variety and movement, being free to wander and explore and meet new people and see new things.

Sagittarius is the sign of esoteric wisdom and higher learning, so being out in the world finding out about other cultures, different religions, other people's points of view, the ways people live, ancient writings, and philosophies inspires and stimulates their senses. Throw in a bit of travel and adventure and they are happy bunnies.

They may be unreliable and hard to pin down, but they are also warm, cheerful, and friendly and always have an open door. Sagittarians have friends from all walks of life, often from many different countries, and prefer to keep a busy schedule. An empty day is anathema to them. Heaven is a place to be at any given hour, preferably all different.

This sign is renowned for their honesty. In a world of fake praise, it's refreshing to know someone speaks the truth. But honesty can hurt. Sometimes others don't want the blunt truth, yet this is the one sign unable to clothe their words in the niceties we all expect. Sometimes it is refreshing; sometimes painful. Fire signs are action-takers, and although deeply intuitive, they are rarely compassionate, so it's unlikely Sagittarius will care much if they tread on someone's sensitive toes.

Like all the mutable signs, they are quite capable of starting down one path and switching direction halfway through, and they resist being tied down. Family life and a mortgage might seem appealing at some stage, but being in the same place with the same person for a lifetime is not easy or natural for them. A sensible partner will give them room to roam, but perhaps a large house and garden would do instead, with a spacious study and at least one wall full of travel books or enlightening subjects. If age or illness necessitates staying put, Sagittarians will still travel in their minds by taking up new studies.

The best careers for Sagittarius involve anything to do with travel and other cultures: travel writer, foreign correspondent, university lecturer, historian, antiquarian, language teacher, and archaeologist are all perfect occupations.

Even if they don't aspire to work in one of these fields, Sagittarians will have a natural curiosity and display their restless need for freedom of movement.

A stable bank balance and a consistent routine are two things Sagittarius has no need of. The most important thing for them is a full, happy, exciting, adventurous life. If a potential partner wants that kind of life too, they should hitch their star to Sagittarius's heart and hold on tight—it might be a bumpy ride, but it will be oh so much fun.

QUICK SUMMARY OF SAGITTARIUS

The archer, who shoots out numerous arrows. Forever trying new ideas and actions. Aims to find the truth of life via new experiences and knowledge. Enjoys travel, intellectual discussions, adventures, foreign languages and cultures, esoteric subjects, religious beliefs, and new knowledge. Mutable, meaning constantly changing and moving, so hard to pin down. Brutally honest and frank, straightforward in dealings with people, but untrustworthy because of their inconsistency. Risk-takers. Often gamble, even if it's just tossing a coin to see which country to go to next. Never deliberately cruel or unkind; nevertheless, they have a tendency to step on people's toes on their way to a new adventure. Has many friends from all over the world, and their interests spread far and wide. Not good at long-term relationships. Needs personal freedom and constant movement. Straight-talking candour is tough to take.

♑
SUN IN CAPRICORN

Motivation and Element: Cardinal earth

Symbol: The goat

Ruled by: Saturn

Sun Sign Dates: December 22 to January 19

Positive Traits: Ambitious, traditional, financially driven, self-disciplined

Negatives: Overly serious, workaholic, status conscious

This is one of the most ambitious of the astrological signs. Capricorn's ruler is Saturn, a stern planet that creates obstacles wherever it is placed in a chart. Saturn's restrictions are considered our life lessons, so Capricorn natives often live a karmic life, more so than any other sign. In other words, it will not be an easy ride. Because of this, they are given the qualities of perseverance, ambition, staying power, and determination. Their sign is cardinal, too, so they are gifted with the ability to overcome obstacles and move forward.

Capricorn's symbol is the goat, who, with its eye on the highest rock, treads its path slowly and sure-footedly, weaving in and out but always heading upward. This accurately describes their constant need to better themselves.

Capricorns have the personal tools to succeed. Working hard is second nature. From an early age they form their ambitions, and these will not be lowly. Capricorns want to stand on that top pinnacle, so they aim high: ruling the country, being head of a prestigious organisation, advising financial institutions. Any situation that provides copious material benefits along with the possibility of accolades will do. They need—and expect—to achieve something lasting and worthy. Overnight success or passing stardom are of no interest. The endgame is everything, even if it takes a lifetime to achieve.

For most Capricorns, success comes late in life, but they don't mind how long it takes as long as they eventually get there. It goes against the grain for them to sit about idly. Capricorns never waste time because they want to see their family name writ large in the history books. They also have a need to justify themselves, so an impressive title or job description makes them feel their life is worthwhile.

Like everything they undertake, Capricorns seeks the best, so they choose a partner with care. It must be someone equally grounded who will not ruin all Capricorn has built, someone who will continue to build alongside them. Capricorn doesn't want a flashy, attractive, glamorous partner, but instead seeks someone smart, tidy, decent, and sensible who will know how to behave when Capricorn eventually becomes president!

Tradition is incredibly important to Capricorn. Having a family, ditto. What is the point of all that hard work and effort unless their children benefit? Their children will be given a first-class education, the best they can afford, and their house will be in a prestigious area—or at the very least, on the edge of one. Capricorn always has an eye on the best house in town and intends to live there one day. Whatever personal sacrifices are necessary are of no importance; they will do what it takes. They are absolutely implacable in their determination to succeed.

This overriding focus on the material aspects of life and the long hours they work means Capricorn does come across as dull to others. They make self-discipline an art form, so others rarely get the chance to socialise with them; Capricorns feel uncomfortable at social events unless they're networking. They will do their best and be polite, but they won't waste time on socialites or lightweights. They will be more tolerant toward those who might take their advice and use it wisely, but it has to be said, they do have a hard-hearted streak that can make them calculating. Their eye is always on power and success.

Mostly, they just plod on, but occasionally the enormity of their task overwhelms them. Saturn is always sitting on their shoulder telling them to be sensible, and he can transform into the famed black dog of depression. Is it any wonder, when Capricorn's task is life-long? Partners and friends should drag them away from work now and then to remind them there is a life outside their office. They will never be a party lover, but Capricorn might appreciate a hike in the hills or a nice meal out. We all need downtime.

If partners manage to get Capricorn to switch off from work, they may catch a glimpse of that very dry sense of humour that pops up now and then. It will be totally unexpected, and often very funny. Even their jokes are clever and worthy, and they will probably be repeated down the years!

QUICK SUMMARY OF CAPRICORN

Ruled by Saturn and has the goat as their symbol. Cautious, reserved, shy, but capable of great personal sacrifice and abstemiousness while making their way in the world. Capable of great persistence in the face of adversity, especially if it will lead to greatness. Aims to succeed in whatever field they choose. Tends to excel; status is what they are after. Wants a grand house, money in secure investments, and to be recognised at work. Practical. Applies themselves. Extremely supportive and protective of their children, and will put them on the road to success with a good education and every advantage possible. Generally lives to a great age with a wiry, strong constitution. Tradition is important, so they follow the rules and need a family to inherit their wealth. Can suffer from depression because of their inability to leave work behind.

≈
SUN IN AQUARIUS

Motivation and Element: Fixed air

Symbol: The water carrier

Ruled by: Uranus

Sun Sign Dates: January 20 to February 18

Positive Traits: Individual, quirky, sociable, friendly, nonjudgmental

Negatives: Unreliable, freedom-loving, emotionally cool

Aquarians are an enigma, and that's just the way they like it. Ruled by the unpredictable planet Uranus, nothing about them is a given. Describing one is a bit like trying to catch a bit of cloud: reach out and there is nothing there, even though it is visible.

They enjoy being unusual, and they don't care one bit what others think. When things get dull, Aquarius's response is to liven things up with an outrageous or shocking remark. Then they stand back and watch how people respond. Aquarians just adore watching life, and that is pretty much how they live—as an observer of human nature rather than a participant. They are objective and aloof in all situations.

Being an air sign, they are cool and detached, calm and logical. They often prefer being with a group of friends rather than one-on-one, and their agreeable, nonjudgmental, accepting nature makes this easy.

From a young age, Aquarians surround themselves with waifs and strays. The more unusual someone is—the more of an outcast they seem—the more Aquarius will feel the need to befriend them. It is unlikely that Aquarius will understand their own motivation… Does Aquarius "adopt" people because of their famed humanitarian bent, or do they just want to see everyone else's reaction? It's not because Aquarius feels sorry for outcasts, because Aquarians don't relate to people in an empathic way. More than likely, they befriend others out of curiosity.

For Aquarius, life is one big experiment fuelled by curiosity. They take action or say controversial things, then stand back to watch the fallout. Aquarians often wonder why people get so upset by everything. To Aquarius, other people are like players on a stage, or a circus parade. They watch with a detached curiosity, intrigued by how others react.

Career-wise, Aquarians employ the same casual attitude. If they get stressed, it certainly doesn't show. Aquarius can comfortably work in big organisations, handling people and meetings while still being relaxed and friendly to everyone from the janitor to the boss. They think outside the box (and always have), which is why they are often considered geniuses, because a genius needs to think obliquely, and they do this naturally. If Aquarius succeeds in a career, it will be more by accident than design, and they don't give a hoot if they get any awards, accolades, or even pay increases. Money and security are like everything else in their life: a curiosity. Somehow or another they manage life just fine, though if a kind colleagues sees one of their brilliant designs, let's hope they grab it and patent it for them. In truth, Aquarius won't care either way. They are the eccentrics of the zodiac and delight in doing things differently from everyone else.

Faults? Of course they have them. Winging it is one of them—especially when they've been asked to give a keynote speech and haven't bothered to write down a single word. This will either lead to something excruciatingly bad or something brilliant. Either way, Aquarius will shrug. They do this in every aspect of life, including relationships: everything is by the seat of their pants, because that's how they like it—it's far more fun!

Stubborn is another fault. Aquarius's motivation is fixed, which is odd for an air sign. Ever tried to contain air? What this means is their personal freedom is inviolate and non-negotiable, and they won't change that for love nor money.

Once Aquarius has made a decision, they won't budge. Appeals to their better nature will fall on stony ground. It is hard to negotiate with someone who doesn't care about the outcome.

Rebellion is within them, and the bizarre and unusual resonate in their souls. Yet, they live life lightly and let others be, so even if Aquarians cannot be all things to all people, at least they are totally true to themselves.

QUICK SUMMARY OF AQUARIUS

Likes everyone and makes no moral judgments. Adopts waifs and strays all their life. Enjoys shocking people. Totally independent, eccentric, and original. Rarely supportive, having little emotional connection or understanding of how others feel. Looks above and beyond the human condition and rarely considers how others view them. Aims to lead a completely different life than is expected. Always manages to do something unique and surprising. Original, unpredictable, and unreliable. Stubborn, because their sign is fixed. Lives life in their own way and will not be tied down. Their clothing or appearance will typically be different and unusual in some way. Fun and friendly, but they head for the exit if things get too stressful or if people get too demanding.

♓
SUN IN PISCES

Motivation and Element: Mutable water

Symbol: The fish

Ruled by: Neptune

Sun Sign Dates: February 19 to March 20

Positive Traits: Kind, gentle, empathic, compassionate, understanding, adaptable

Negatives: Unreliable, too dreamy, retreats in the face of stress, snappy and irritable when overfaced

Pisces is a gentle sign, sweet and receptive, kind and supportive. Others admire their understanding and compassion. But life is not just a conversation and a supportive hug—it is about exams and jobs and driving on busy freeways and the hustle-bustle of modern life, packed shops, dog-eat-dog ambitions, and vying to be (and have) the best. All this leaves Pisces reeling. It's as if they are standing in a calm oasis in the middle of a fast-forwarded image of life: cars and people, noise and chaos. That is how they experience life, wide-eyed and in shock. Sometimes they feel they have come from another planet, because the way we live now is so out far of Pisces's comfort zone that they find it hard to function.

Pisces is a mutable water sign. Water signs are about feelings, emotions, and empathy with others. Mutable means changeable, so they are people of changeable emotions, and they have flexibility in their thoughts and actions. Usually, this is seen as a positive, but they have no other base. That is the whole of Pisces: a sweet, kind, gentle bundle of receptivity and compassion. They don't have the practical tools for today's world because that would involve stamina, of which they have a limited amount.

And life requires decision-making, which is not Pisces's forte. Why is that? Because their symbol is the fish—two fish swimming in opposite directions. Think of each as an idea or possibility. Here comes one, and yes, that seems good—but then along comes the other fish from the opposite direction, and that idea seems good too. How can they decide when they understand all points of view, when they see the whole picture and, most of the time, something even bigger than that? How can they decide on anything when they resonate with the entirety of humanity? It's no wonder Pisceans struggle with decisions and the fast pace of life. It is alien to them in every way.

That is why many Pisceans have creative talents: they are artists, writers, potters, fashion designers, musicians, and filmmakers. They tuck themselves away in a studio or shed so they can do what they do best without having to face that crazy world out there, and they strive to be creative in whatever way provides peaceful self-expression. Words are difficult for Pisceans unless they are imaginative. It is hard enough to see the whole picture without trying to verbalise it; it's far easier to live in a make-believe world they create for themselves. Most Pisceans are psychic, but like everything else about them, their psychic abilities are an ethereal, slippery thing, and they can get confused as to whether they had a true vision or if it was just their imagination playing tricks.

Pisces ebbs and flows, tossed this way and that by their prevailing moods and the emotions of their loved ones. Although they are willing to take on all the troubles of those they care for, Pisceans are often unable to. Escapism is their route to personal sanity, and they often drift into dreams, their imagination, or, sometimes, alcohol and drugs. The world is a tough place for Pisceans. People are unkind, man's inhumanity to his fellow man is incomprehensible, and they often struggle to cope.

Vulnerable, shy, charitable, kind, and understanding, Pisceans should look for a partner who is earthy and practical, but who also comprehends their true nature and allows them to float away on their river of emotions now and then. There is no doubt that their partner will be the mainstay in every area of their lives because Pisces lives in a muddle emotionally, physically, and mentally. But if someone takes them on, in return Pisces will be there for them no matter what, ready with a sympathetic ear and supportive hug. Anything more is beyond them.

QUICK SUMMARY OF PISCES

Sensitive, dreamy, compassionate, understanding, and sympathetic. Also unreliable, emotionally cool, and extremely vulnerable. Not really equipped for life as we know it. Unnerved by stress and pressure. Upset by the fast pace of life. Exhausted by too many demands. Has limited energy and is always looking for an escape route from life's difficulties, which is why so many seek oblivion in alcohol and/or drugs. Capable of great perception; they know if someone is unhappy or in trouble. Naturally provides support and a sympathetic ear, but they cannot sustain that for long. Cannot shoulder responsibility. Slips away to calmer waters when things get to be too much. Ideal jobs are those that do not involve any stress or deadlines. Are often artists because they can work alone and express their deep and varied feelings. Many have a clairvoyant bent.

two
MOON SIGNS

The moon is a powerful planet that rules our emotions. It's fast-moving, passing through each astrological sign approximately every two days, which is why we can't assign exact dates to the moon as we can the sun. If you don't know your moon sign, pull up your birth chart to find out. The symbol for the moon is a crescent, so it should be easy to find.

Our moon sign describes how we relate to other people, what makes us feel emotionally safe and secure, and what nurtures us. Generally, a high percentage of happy relationships involve people who share sun and moon signs. If our moon sign is the same as our partner's sun sign and vice versa, it is easy to appreciate each other's emotions, feelings, and drive. Because they naturally have similar tendencies, partners are able to understand each other's behaviours.

If this ideal pairing isn't possible, the sun and moon being in the same element is helpful. If our moon is in an earth sign—Taurus, Virgo, or Capricorn—we relate more easily to other earth moons because both moons want the same thing: stability and security. Fire moons—Aries, Leo, and Sagittarius—will enjoy being active together and may share a love of an exciting sport. Water moons—Cancer, Scorpio, and Pisces—understand each other's need for emotional support and tenderness and will be protective of each other's sensitivities. Air moons—Gemini, Libra, and Aquarius—will enjoy discussing things with their mates, often chatting late into the night.

People whose moon signs are incompatible rarely get together. It does happen, of course, and usually because there is some other compelling aspect to the person. However, these relationships rarely last unless one of the other important planets (Mercury, Venus, or Mars) is in the same astrological sign as their partner's moon.

Incompatible moons are usually fire and water because water douses the flames of fire, so the water moon will suppress the fire moon's emotions. Earth and fire moons may also have a problem because the speed with which fire makes emotional decisions is scary to earth moons;

earth moons will feel equally wary of air moons for a similar reason: their changeable unreliability. Air and water moons have difficulties because the air moon only likes *talking* about emotions and is wary of the depths of emotion shown by the water moon, so the water moon will feel misunderstood and unfulfilled. Water moons are so deeply sensitive that other moon signs find it difficult to fulfil their needs. However, if other elements between couples are good, even incompatible moons can be overcome with tolerance and understanding on both sides.

When we decide we like someone, it is usually before we know the details of their birth chart, so we use an innate, subconscious antennae to pick up on their attitudes and feelings. If their personality resonates within us, we take the relationship further. In these instances of immediate connection, I encourage you to check both birth charts. I'd be willing to bet that either the sun and moon signs, or both moon signs, will be compatible.

ARIES MOON
Fire/Water Combination
Positive Traits: Emotionally warm, affectionate, happy

Negatives: Unfeeling, insensitive, tough, uncompromising

This is not a comfortable combination. The moon is all about feelings, so therefore it is happier in a water sign, where it can express its emotional quality. In the cardinal fire of Aries, the moon becomes a little unfeeling and insensitive. Like everything Aries does, this is not intentional, and they certainly do not mean to be unkind, but they don't waste time on people who turn out not to be right for them. They are also easily bored and like emotional excitement, which does not bode well for long-term relationships.

Those with an Aries moon are emotionally direct, honest, and quick. They see someone and head straight over to ask them out on a date, and no amount of wise advice from others is heeded. Their sights have been set on a target and nothing will deter them. And it's easy for others to fall in love with Aries. With their confident, cheerful, honest manner, prospective partners find them hard to resist. They are generous with their time, energy, and money, so holidays, short breaks, and exciting adventures await partners at the start. Being warm-hearted, hugs come naturally with an Aries moon.

Once the initial magic in a relationship starts fading, their interest may wane. If partners are overly emotional or get depressed, if they are too demanding of Aries' time, if they expect Aries to drop everything to do something they want, or if they start accusing Aries of selfishness and the inability to compromise (both of which are probably true), this moon sign will be heading for the door.

It is not that Aries doesn't care, but they don't like to be told what to do and how to live their life—not even by the person they love. Nor do they have the ability to fit in with others, as they prefer to be independent. If their loved one starts crying, Aries will give them a hug and a few words of advice, but if their partner doesn't quickly recover, irritation and frustration will rise in Aries. They expect everyone to do as they do when upset: find a new focus.

Aries is a courageous, active sign. It is resilient and straight-talking. As a moon sign, this creates a certain amount of insensitivity when it comes to the gentler arts of love. Subtlety is not their forte; romance is often lost on them. A nice meal at a restaurant is fine. Talking about their new business over dinner? Great. But back home, Aries will either make love in a fast, perfunctory fashion and then insist on watching something on the television, or they'll head to their desk to work. Either way, the romance will come and go pretty fast, so it is best Aries aligns themselves with someone who doesn't expect to cry on their shoulder all night, who doesn't need more than a quick hug, who has plenty of things to do themselves, and who doesn't rely too much on them.

Aries moons are emotionally independent people, and it will save a lot of heartache if they choose a cooler air sign partner who is similarly inclined, or even a placid earth sign. Certainly, it is advisable to steer clear of the water signs, as they are far too sensitive and easily upset for an Aries moon. They are modern in their approach, preferring partners to be independent too so that they meet as equals. Aries never likes leaners, and as a moon sign, it is emotionally fragile people they cannot cope with.

Once Aries realises a relationship isn't going to work, they are able to say so, and they leave. Guilt is not part of their emotional makeup. They can accept the inevitable, and their innate optimism assures them there are plenty more fish in the sea. And anyway, Aries can manage just fine alone if necessary. There is a toughness about Aries moons, an implacable side, that blocks the finer feelings when it comes to their emotions.

Being the first sign of the zodiac, Aries' needs come first. Compromise is an alien concept to them. Their partners might despair of them in many ways, but Aries will still adore them after fifty years if their partners allow them to be the irrepressible, independent, and warm person an Aries moon truly is.

TAURUS MOON
Earth/Water Combination

Positive Traits: Emotionally steady, reliable, trustworthy, safe

Negatives: Unchanging, stubborn, lacks sensitivity

The moon works quite well in Taurus. It is not emotional, which the moon prefers, but it *is* safe. This is because Taurus is an earth sign, so it is stable. Taurus's sign is the bull, and we all know nothing moves a bull. Emotionally, that is what Taurus moons are like: reliable and safe and slow to change. Ideally, they prefer never to change partners once they've made a commitment. When they fall in love, it is usually forever.

But, like everything Taurus does, making that commitment takes time. Even when they have selected their life partner, they wait. Rushing in and declaring love is not for them. Taurus wants something to offer this person, something to lure them in, so they take it step by step. They get a good job, work hard, and save their money. This fixed earth sign does things the old-fashioned way on the premise that if it worked for the generations who came before, it will work for them. And they are unlikely to choose a flighty or unsuitable person because, having spent years building, the last thing Taurus wants is someone frittering away everything they've worked for. So, they take their time deciding on a partner, but once their mind is made up, there is no telling them no.

Taurus will go after this person implacably determined to win them, and Taurus moons never give up. Very often, they wear down the person's resistance with their dogged persistence; there is something appealing about someone who is so devoted and unchanging. We all feel we deserve love, and when Taurus goes courting, their loved one will feel very special indeed.

The partner of a Taurus moon can expect all the trappings of a secure life, but they may, in the end, feel like one of Taurus's belongings. It has to be said: Taureans are a tad possessive. Their life partner is viewed very much like everything else Taurus has extended effort gaining—that person is *theirs*.

When in love, Taurus adores their partner. Being a tactile, earthy person, they enjoy the physical aspects of the partnership: cuddling up together, eating and drinking, making love. All earth signs like nature, so Taurus moons enjoy walking with loved ones, swimming, hiking, or any other pastime that fills their senses with the sights and sounds of the great outdoors and the contentment of sharing it with the one they care for.

To lure a Taurus moon, others need to attend to the practical aspects: get a good job, save their money, learn to rustle up a delicious meal or two, make sure the places they go on dates are sensuous (like a spa or beautiful nature spot), wear perfume/aftershave, dress in clothes that are appealing to touch, talk about future plans that are sensible and grounded, and never turn their back on them in bed. If they do all of that, they'll most likely have a Taurus moon eating right out of their hand!

If a Taurus moon suspects a rival, they won't make a fuss, cry, scream, or rant and rave. They will wait—it might be a passing fancy. They never overreact or take hasty action. But if a partner decides to leave, Taurus will be stunned into immobility. Time will be required to assimilate and accept the situation. To do that, they take it day by day and put one foot in front of the other. Gradually, the pain dulls, and then they start again, looking to build another nest. They won't be crying on the phone to a friend, but they may down a bottle or two of wine before accepting things and moving on.

The problem is, Taurus's love, once given, is like everything else in their life: long-term and lasting. They rarely stop loving someone years after they have gone. So, it's wise not to break their heart. Just because Taurus appears calm and unruffled does not mean they don't have deep feelings. No one else will ever love as deeply and as adoringly as them, so let's hope others think very hard before walking away; the rest of the signs are lightweights in comparison.

GEMINI MOON
Air/Water Combination

Positive Traits: Fun, friendly, chatty, witty, bonds easily with others by finding shared interests

Negatives: Emotionally unreliable, changeable, lacks empathy

Gemini is an air sign, and air signs are cerebral and unemotional. That does not mean they don't care about others; it means they are logical and able to rationalise situations, even those that are personal. They have the ability to act sensibly even when they lose something or someone they love, which is a rare quality. To others (particularly to water signs, who are deeply emotional), this might come across as unfeeling, but it is simply another way of handling emotional issues.

Every sign reacts differently to the life situations we all face. Gemini moons have the ability to move forward by shrugging off pain. They have an innate understanding that too much emotion can be detrimental to psychological health. Gemini moons do fall in love and make commitments; they do marry and have children. But they do it with a clear vision that is not clouded by overwhelming emotions.

Gemini moon's decisions are logical. They actively dislike being around dramatic people who are moody or self-pitying; they hate anything taken to extremes. A Gemini moon's way of handling life is to tell a joke to lighten the atmosphere. They have a charming glibness that can find humour in any situation, even when they're facing the very worst.

While the sign of Gemini is not renowned for its empathy, when the moon is in this sign they are happy to listen to other people's problems, but they will do so with a cool, assessing logic and then suggest solutions: something they once heard; something someone said who faced a similar situation. They recall everything and delight in having an answer. As long as the discussion does not dissolve into an emotional morass, Gemini moons can handle it. But if there are tears, accusations, complaints, or drama, they will flee the scene. Explain a problem clearly and calmly and a Gemini moon often surprises with their astute observations.

They connect to people through conversation, so they often fall in love with people's minds before their bodies. It is the enjoyment of conversation that keeps them committed. The moment a loved one loses interest in bantering and discussing things, Gemini will often lose interest in them. They simply must have a meeting of minds, even into old age.

So, they are not overly emotional, they don't get dramatic and demanding, and they don't try to manipulate people and situations. They give people space by allowing the winds of freedom to blow in a relationship. This gives Gemini moons the ability to be good friends with their partners, to discuss problems without emotions clouding the issue, and to move forward in life even during the bad times.

Their youthful enthusiasm for life in the present moment—not as it once was, or as what it might be in the future—means Gemini moons effortlessly live in the now. They are one of the few signs who embrace cultural changes. They don't long for the past and how it used to be, which is why they are eternally youthful in their outlook. No matter what age they are, it is essential for their inner happiness that Gemini moons are right in the middle of things, enjoying the moment as it happens, and being part of the group who make it happen.

A Gemini moon is the same person with their friends and their lovers. Nothing about them is disguised. They accept their partner's life choices and encourage them to try new things. To their children, Gemini moons are a friend, full of fun ideas for days out. Gemini moons are never too parentally demanding or strict, and they use humour to deliver their messages. They may not hug as much as much as some parents, but their kids will turn to them when they need advice.

Of course, Gemini moons aren't perfect. No one is. Gemini is the sign of the twins, which means they have two sides to their personality. Like everyone else, there are times when their good humour deserts them, when they feel tired and stuck. That's when the other twin appears, the one who can be snappy and critical. Gemini's cleverness with language means they have a waspish, satirical tongue when hurt. And we all have times in life when we seek emotional reassurance from our partners, but Gemini moons find it hard to give this support. So, they aren't all things to all people—but then again, no one is.

Like everything about them, their bad moods are fleeting. They are rarely down for long. And a Gemini moon never holds on to pain or hurt, so can easily forgive and forget. They want life to be light and fun again, so they do their best to bring that about, because that is the situation in which they can truly be themselves.

If a potential partner seeks an intense relationship, a Gemini moon won't be interested. They live life lightly, leave few footsteps, and bring happiness wherever they go, and if that isn't a gift, I don't know what is.

CANCER MOON
Water/Water Combination

Positive Traits: Emotionally caring, sympathetic, understanding, supportive

Negatives: Overly emotional, ultrasensitive to remarks and situations, temperamental

The moon rules Cancer, so it finds its perfect home here, where it can express all of its deep and varied feelings. Cancerians are therefore full of empathy and consideration for others, and they're able to relate to people at every level. Often, they choose a caring profession: many sun and moon Cancerians are in the medical field or in a healing profession. Being sympathetic listeners, they also make great counsellors; their natural empathy is so strong that complete strangers often confess to them. Cancer is intuitive to the feelings of others and would never knowingly hurt anyone, and people can sense this.

The main priority for anyone with an important planet in Cancer (especially the moon) is emotional security. Despite their courageous and bold life helping others, inside they are extremely vulnerable to cruel words or personal injustices. If someone says something that hurts, they are stunned. Having given so much of themselves in every way, to be verbally attacked shocks them to the core. Cancer's symbol is the crab, and a crab wears its shell as a protection. This accurately describes the sign's emotional vulnerability.

Cancer really does relate to every injustice in the world. Man's inhumanity to his fellow man is incomprehensible to them. Why can't people stop fighting and start caring for each other? Some are so overwhelmed they won't read the news, instead choosing to focus on their close family.

The number one aim of a Cancer moon is finding emotional security via a supportive partner who truly understands their inner sensitivities. Cancer moons need a partner who comprehends their need to be constantly reassured that although others may have betrayed them, they never will. Cancer needs to be able to talk to their partner about their emotions and their feelings, so they seek a receptive, supportive, kind person to share their lives with—someone who makes them feel safe and secure.

But for Cancer, finding love is a minefield because of their emotional susceptibility. Crying is second nature. Everything brings tears to their eyes, but nothing more so than being hurt by someone they trusted. They never forget what they perceive as an injustice, so each new rejection adds to their insecurity.

Being ruled by the moon gives them changeable emotions. One minute they can be happy, the next sad. Because they are ultrasensitive to any offhand remarks, loved ones and family have to tread lightly to avoid upsetting them. Friends, too, can easily offend a Cancer moon if they don't immediately support and agree with them. Yet, it is this same emotional sensitivity that makes them such kind, supportive friends and partners. No one is a more caring and genuinely supportive partner and friend than a Cancer moon. They are always available for the ones they love; they give their time and energy freely, without counting the cost. Yes, Cancer moons expect total attention from others, but they give total attention in return.

It is rare to find a lone Cancer moon. Having a partner and a family is part of who they are. Expressing their caring nature always starts with their closest family and friends and spreads outward into the world, and without this outlet they cannot be who they truly are. Their friends and family are of the utmost importance.

While they're keen to keep in touch with distant family, if there isn't a reciprocal effort, Cancer moons will give up on them. As they age, Cancer moons become more selective of who they are supportive of. This often means they have fewer friends, but those friends have stood the test of time; Cancer knows they are there for them through thick and thin.

Family gatherings are when Cancer moons feel most at peace. There is nothing more fulfilling for them than watching everyone eating and laughing together. Their beloved family knows that Cancer's love and care will always be there for them, and that it is a prize worth more than gold—which is the colour of their heart.

LEO MOON

Fire/Water Combination

Positive Traits: Emotionally warm, affectionate, tactile, adores being in love

Negatives: Bossy, easily influenced by the glamorous life, expects constant attention or will look elsewhere

Ruled by the sun itself, Leos glow with animal magnetism. Their symbol is the lion for a reason. It accurately describes Leo's personality: the way they look after their pride and cubs, keeping all danger at bay, making sure they have available food and resources, sheltering them from danger by fighting foes on their behalf.

Warm and affectionate, Leo moons are capable of giving a lot to their partners and family, but they really need to receive appreciation and praise for their efforts, which are considerable—they expect those they care for to understand and appreciate all they do for them. Leo needs thanks. And the more thanks they get, the more Leo does in return. It rouses them to greater efforts.

Leos moons are all in love with love. Being a fire sign, their emotions and passions are quickly aroused. In public, they beeline to a person they like the look of. Bold and courageous, Leo moons will have no problem setting up a date; few people can resist a Leo on a mission.

Romance brings out the best in them. Being in love is the best time of their life. Because they seek high drama, nothing is more pleasing than passionate encounters, and they love when their partner gazes adoringly at them. Leo moons instinctively know how to love and be loved, and they are experts at romance and the subtle arts of seduction. Plus, they are generous to the extreme. To be fair, they never baulk at spending money, both on themselves and on the one they love, so they never forget birthdays or anniversaries. But woe betide a partner who forgets about their Leo!

It delights them to dress up and go out somewhere special. Leo knows all the best places because they have a desire for the high life, and they adore being in the same place as the rich and famous. Even if Leo doesn't aspire to celebrity status, on holiday they enjoy nothing more than strutting their stuff down an avenue frequented by the rich—and with their innate style and charisma, they could easily pass for one of them behind those dark sunglasses. Leo is the sign of the actor, who craves being the centre of attention, so even if it's only make-believe while on holiday, they revel in pretending and having fun. They always have an eye on the mirror and how they look.

Fire signs tend to put their own needs first, and certainly Leo can be egotistical. This means they cannot handle being criticised at all. Quite the reverse! They require constant affirmation: how wonderful they are, how attractive, how generous, how brave. No amount of praise will ever be too much, and if Leo's partner doesn't always put them and their needs first, they can feel very neglected. But even a partner who adores their Leo might get tired of having to praise them all the time, especially in a long-term relationship when work and family issues take a great deal of their time. Leo moons will take no prisoners because they cannot accept this. Having extended so much energy and effort, if people ignore all they do and forget to thank them, inside Leo will feel deeply wounded—despite being too proud to show they care. And although the sign of Leo is fixed (and therefore they prefer staying with one partner), if they don't feel fully appreciated, they will look elsewhere: the ball will be firmly in their partner's court as to whether Leo stays or goes.

Leo moons often enjoy the company of children because they have that enthusiastic, childlike love of entertainment: plays, circuses, amusement parks, days out—they are more than happy to have a go at anything. With their sparkling good humour, they make everything enjoyable.

Given how much they do for loved ones, Leo thinks a bit of praise is not much to ask. All they want is to be truly loved and adored, and to enjoy a life full of emotion and passion. Leo lives life as if it's a play and they have the starring role; if not given the spotlight at all times, they will leave.

Those who know a Leo moon will understand how charismatic they are. When Leo enters a room, it's as if a light has been switched on. Their warmth and charm is like the glow of the sun. They are certainly demanding, but it's worth it, because if Leo gives up and departs, partners will definitely feel a dimming of the light.

VIRGO MOON

Earth/Water Combination

Positive Traits: Emotionally committed to one partner, reliable, sexy

Negatives: Extremely selective and fussy, critical of loved ones, waspish tongue

The modest enigma, Virgo. Underneath that slightly prudish, fussy exterior lurks a very warm, sensuous, and passionate person. Surprised? Do you know some Virgos who don't seem passionate at all? That's because, on the surface, Virgo doesn't look sexy. Their innate modesty means they dress conservatively. They see being showy as crass—and they really do hate the obvious. Virgo likes class, and they wear it well whatever it is, but it won't be obviously sexy or inviting.

Emotionally, they are hard to please because they expect partners to be clean and tidy and to look after themselves, just as they do. Virgo moons are very keen on following a good diet and regular exercise, and they would feel uncomfortable with someone who couldn't care less about how they look, who never considered their health, who dripped soup all down their front, or who dropped biscuit crumbs in their lap. People who are slovenly in their habits and/or dress won't get to first base with a Virgo moon because it would drive them nuts.

It's all part of keeping things tidy, which is their main aim in life: tidying up messes. Virgo starts with themselves, their diet, and their clothes. Then the focus moves on to their partner, family, house, and car, then the office, and then other people—in that order. Virgo's laser eye misses nothing, not even a speck of dust, and they simply cannot ignore it and walk on by.

It gets very tiring, and there is only so much one person can do, but Virgo still worries and frets and fusses about the jobs that haven't been done. And when they nitpick and criticise and moan, people don't like it—none of us like criticism. Because of Virgo's habit of looking for more work once a job has been completed, partners might have to tell them to stop working and drag them away.

So, getting a Virgo moon into the mood might be their partner's hardest task. However, if they pour a drink, dim the lights (so their Virgo can't see the stuff that needs to be done), play soft music, and talk quietly, that laser eye might be temporarily dimmed. In the end, Virgos are logical, and they know they are their own worst enemy with work and details and fussiness, so it is lovely to be told to sit, drink, and relax. They will take a deep breath and allow the day's cares to flow out of them, and then their passionate nature will become obvious.

Of course, life soon reasserts itself, so it won't be long before Virgo is writing a shopping list in their head, deciding how much they are willing to pay to have the windows replaced, or another similarly dull but pressing problem they have been considering.

For Virgo, finding that perfect someone to share their life with is not easy. When someone asks them out, they are inclined to think that person is just being kind. If the person persists, Virgo will accept—as long as they are clean, neat, and tidy. If their date is also trustworthy and reliable, they might consider bestowing their heart, but they will take time over the decision. What if they get let down or their trust is abused? It is hard for Virgo to accept that someone adores them, and since they play for keeps, they don't want to make any mistakes.

Once committed, Virgo moons make fabulous partners. They're hardworking, dutiful, and kind, with that earthy sexuality hidden underneath. No matter what tasks life throws at them, Virgo adds the task to their list and gets it done. But yes, they do have a moan now and then. Children might find their Virgo parent extra fussy; a Virgo parent might insist nothing is eaten in the car because they don't want to hoover up the crumbs, or they might complain the washing isn't where it should be (in the basket!), but the kids will be loved and looked after. Children with Virgo parents are given good, healthy, nutritious food, and their school clothes/sports kit will always be ironed, folded, and ready on the exact day they are needed.

Virgo moons aren't wild, showy, impulsive, or fiery. They are gentle, kind, modest people who really care and who really help, and those that they bestow their love to should consider themselves blessed.

LIBRA MOON
Air/Water Combination

Positive Traits: Emotionally cool, calm, collected, attractive, peace-loving, compromises easily

Negatives: Wants only the best, cares about appearances (and partner's financial status), capable of using others

Ruled by Venus, the planet of love, it is a given that relationships are the most important aspect of a Libra moon's life. In a birth chart, Libra also rules the area of partnerships, so their whole life is geared to finding a partner (both at work and at home) to go through life with.

Having said that, Libra moons have high and exacting standards. Libra is an air sign, so they use logic when choosing a partner. Love is all well and good, but they require something extra, and that is class. Their cool, calm, refined manner needs a mate who is able to suggest nice places to go and who looks as good as them.

With Venus as their ruling planet, Libra is bound to be beautiful (or attractive at the very least), and the arts of seduction come naturally to them. They know just how to flirt and woo and tease, and with those dimples or the way they raise an eyebrow, they manage to convey exactly the right message without being coarse in any way.

People who are ugly, rude, or vulgar frighten them and are avoided, which is why those ruled by Venus often look for someone wealthy—so they can experience a life removed from those rougher elements. And with their charm, style, and elegance, it is often easy to find the right partner.

Does this sound a bit contrived? Yes, it is. But Libra is an air sign, so it's cerebral, which means they never allow emotions to cloud the issue, no matter how much in love they are. There is always a bit they hold back, just to make sure they can extricate themselves if life takes a downward turn. When the ship is sinking, Libra moon always dives overboard.

Libra's symbol is the scales. Their life is all about keeping everything in balance, and their astrological purpose is to bring harmony and peace to everyone. Thus, they strive to lead a life that is calm and relaxed. It is easy for them to compromise anything except their need for luxury. With their considerable charm coupled with their impressive intellect, they are more than capable of working hard to provide the lifestyle they require all on their own, but if a mate can bring some extra luxury with them, all the better.

When committed, Libra moon will strive to keep things quiet and gentle. They are innately fair and naturally see both sides of an argument, so they always understand someone else's point of view, and their clever mind will instantly create a compelling and persuasive argument to the contrary. As a result, they always manage to get their own way without even raising their voice.

Those scales can go down as well as up. It is tough keeping everything in balance, always being reasonable and calm, acting as mediator between friends who have fallen out, attending to disputes at work, and creating a nice atmosphere wherever they are. Being only human, Libra needs some time off to recharge their batteries. When they're recharging, Libras have trouble dragging themselves out of bed or attending to the simplest task. It won't be long before they will be out in the world doing their best to create harmony and beauty again, but first, they need downtime to recover their energy levels and their enthusiasm.

Most Libras manage to avoid life's unpleasant and boring jobs by hiring other people to do them, so in an ideal world they would have staff to clean the house, cut the grass, and valet the car. If children come along, they will make full use of nannies and older family members to relieve them of any strain, and they will still manage to head out for an evening of wining and dining. It is rare to see a stressed-out Libra mum or dad. Even when they go through their recharging periods, they still manage to look good despite lounging around on the couch all day: tousled hair only adds to their charm, and that angelic smile can persuade anyone to do anything, so Libra will make full use of someone who pops in to see how they are!

For someone ruled by Venus, they are remarkably cool in close relationships. Too much intensity scares them. Yet, they try to please. Libra moons are lovely partners—always elegant, always classy. But, partners take note: Have a comfortable bank balance and be generous with it, or lovely Libra will be heading to pastures new.

SCORPIO MOON
Water/Water Combination

Positive Traits: Emotionally loyal, passionate, protective, capable

Negatives: Controlling, secretive, manipulative

Deceptively calm and secretive, this sign will not show their feelings to people until they know them well. Even then, Scorpio moons withhold a lot. This is all to do with trust, which does not come easily to them. Being so canny and aware of the ways people manipulate others, they are always on the lookout in case someone is about to expect something Scorpio has no intention of providing. The fact is, emotionally, Scorpio must have control of relationships and prefers others to be dependent on them. So they play cat and mouse all the time, which makes a relationship with them extremely challenging. Also, Scorpio moons are concerned that if others see the depth of their emotions and passions before fully under their spell, their intended might run for cover!

Like a spider in a web, these people are adept at the art of seduction and have no trouble luring in partners. But then, just to make sure others are not being false, Scorpio devises little tests and secret ways of sussing out another's hidden motives; they simply find it impossible to believe others don't have an agenda. If someone is being generous and honest, surely there must be a reason.

Eventually, of course, even a Scorpio moon will have to accept someone loves them. When that happens, they give their all, which is considerable. Being a water sign, their feelings and passions run incredibly deep; their tests were simply to make sure they weren't going to be misled or hurt. Because the depth of Scorpio's love is immeasurable, the pain of rejection would be unbearable, hence their caution. Yet, they have an intense desire to experience oneness with another, and they seek a total blending. There is nothing emotionally light about a Scorpio moon.

Partners, then, will have to be strong, or they can wilt under Scorpio's constantly watchful eye. Deep feelings can give rise to negative emotions, and jealousy and suspicion are Scorpio's worst traits. It's that fear of being hurt and exposed—of someone getting so close they have the power to destroy them—that keeps them forever on their emotional toes, forever alert.

Most people enjoy the initial passion of a new relationship but then expect the drama to die down and be replaced by a comfortable togetherness. A Scorpio moon will have none of that—comfortable togetherness would bore them to death. When their relationship starts getting cosy, they deliberately shake things up by instigating an argument or making an accusation, and so the fun begins again, and they are happy. They want to live a life full of passion and hot feelings, and they have no intention of ever being emotionally calm. So, be warned, this sign expects full-on attention at every turn, and for life!

Once another person has managed to persuade Scorpio they love them like no other, and once Scorpio has given them their heart, Scorpio will defend their partner to the death. Loyal to the nth degree, totally protective and fiercely possessive, if anyone dares to hurt their partner, Scorpio's cold anger is a scary thing to see. That famed sting in Scorpio's tail is not a myth. This sign is both hot and cold, but it is the latter people need to be more afraid of.

Scorpio moons seek someone who can love them deeply, but they cannot have a partner who is a pushover because they would get bored. Ultimately, they need someone clever, intelligent, and grounded with an inner sense of self-worth, who can ride the barrage of tests and trials and emerge smiling. They passed, they survived, and so Scorpio's love is like the deepest ocean: dark, unfathomable, all-consuming, and total. A note to all prospective partners of a Scorpio: think very carefully. They expect and need a lifetime of drama, so brace yourself and take a deep breath before diving into that broiling sea. It is going to be a bumpy ride, because no one will test you, confuse you, control you—or love you—more than a Scorpio moon.

SAGITTARIUS MOON
Fire/Water Combination

Positive Traits: Emotionally spontaneous, fun, adventurous, warm

Negatives: Unreliable, changeable, unpredictable

Like all fire moons, Sagittarians are warm and affectionate, but they cannot cope with overly emotional or needy people. Their affectionate nature is fleeting because this sign is mutable, meaning changeable, and this can cause a few issues when it comes to commitment. Most people eventually settle down, but this will be Sagittarius's greatest challenge because there is nothing stable about moving fire. Like a hillside swept with flames, Sagittarius moons move here and there, depending on the wind, and are often impossible to predict. So it is with their emotions. Being a restless, impulsive, active person, the idea of curtailing their freedom does not appeal in the least. Sagittarius is a wanderer. They need to feel unfettered and free to roam the world, physically or mentally—preferably both. With their irresistible need to explore and experiment, keeping to the straight and narrow will neither appeal nor be feasible in reality.

The archer is Sagittarius's symbol for a reason. Those arrows he shoots out are ideas—and please note, it is *arrows*. Plural. This describes the Sagittarian penchant for scattering their energy across numerous projects and ideas, spreading themselves thin trying to be everywhere, do everything, and learn all there is to know. Intimate relationships are bound to suffer since Sagittarians have a huge group of friends from all walks of life, constant restlessness, and insatiable hunger for knowledge and movement.

Not everyone wants a commitment, of course. And while young, footloose, and fancy-free Sagittarius moons will have lovers and drop them and move on, generally enjoying all that life has to offer without a second thought. Only when they are older might it occur to them that everyone else has found a partner, made a commitment, and had a family. Then, Sagittarius might give it a go. But, in their heart, they are never really committed to anything.

Not only are they impossible to pin down, they are renowned as the most honest and truthful of the astrological signs. Sagittarians do not have the ability to conceal their thoughts and words, so they cannot come up with the niceties we all use to avoid offending others. If people ask a Sagittarius for their opinion, they get the blunt, unvarnished truth. Subconsciously, people are used to being politely lied to, so when Sagittarians say it how it is, it can be a bit shocking.

Another aspect that may cause friction in a relationship is that Sagittarius moons need to have a lot of friends. They cannot be exclusively focused on their partner because learning and exchanging information is Sagittarius's passion. But partners might get a little edgy when Sagittarius spends so much time chatting to others, or when the meal they cooked has gone cold because their partner got so absorbed in a subject they completely forgot the time. When they've had a bit too much to drink at a party, Sagittarians are the type of people who suddenly decide to sleep on their friend's couch, often forgetting to phone home to explain before nodding off. And even the most important of occasions means little to them, so recalling birthdays and anniversaries is a difficult task.

In truth, it won't be difficult to find a partner. A Sagittarius moon's enthusiasm and zest for life is very appealing. When they meet someone who can suggest new adventures, their eyes will light up. They just adore heading off at a moment's notice. They love talking for hours about obscure subjects, and they are quite happy to sleep on floors or under the stars. It is true that their pockets are usually empty, because money is the last thing Sagittarius thinks about. Being ruled by expansive Jupiter, they have an innate feeling that the universe will always support them, or that someone will step in to help. This is the sign of the risk-taker and gambler, and that's how Sagittarius moons live their emotional life: by the seat of their pants.

Sagittarius moons desire the most exciting and adventurous life it is possible to have. If partners have the cash to finance the next expedition, they may well hold onto their adventurous partner for a while, but unless a birth chart has some earth elements to balance a Sagittarius moon, they could be a wandering star all their life.

CAPRICORN MOON
Earth/Water Combination

Positive Traits: Emotionally stable, reliable, trustworthy, committed

Negatives: Workaholic, not overly sympathetic or understanding

As an earth sign, Capricorn moons seek stability in their relationships. Valuing tradition, they certainly desire a partner and a family. Professionally, they always aim high. Capricorn's whole life is geared toward gathering money, property, and as many accolades and awards as possible, but it isn't a selfish desire, it's for the family—not just their own children, but for the generations who come after. Naturally, having a mate and children is essential to their life plan.

This moon sign thinks on a grand scale, but it isn't all idle dreams. They have every intention of achieving their aims, and to that end, they work extremely hard. Nothing sways them from their course. Like Capricorn's symbol, the goat, they want to climb higher and higher, with their eye on being at the top of their profession.

In relationships, then, they look for the very best. Ideally, Capricorn moons have a partner who brings wealth and status to the mix. But, more than that, they desire a partner who has that extra *je ne sais quoi*, because when they reach the dizzy heights of their intended life path, they want to be standing next to a partner who makes them proud. Flighty, superficial people who seek celebrity status will not get to first base with them. Capricorn moons seek a kindred spirit, so their partners will already be secure or—at the very least—also want to build in the long-term. Capricorn doesn't waste the time of day on fly-by-nights.

Being emotionally cool, cautious, reserved, and more than a little old-fashioned in their ideas about what constitutes a suitable partner, prospective partners need to scrub up on their dress, their manners, and their vocabulary. They must know how to hold their knife and fork and how to behave in every circumstance—yes, even in this day and age, Capricorn values the old ways.

Deep inside, Capricorn moons feel a bit inadequate, especially when it comes to matters of the heart. They never have chat-up lines or glib phrases at the ready, and the art of seduction is alien to them. Instead, they offer prospective life partners all they have in material terms and explain what their future aims are.

With that being said, Capricorn moons can fall in love, and do. Their selection process might seem calculating, but they give their all to a partner once they commit. Earth signs seek a forever love. But it is also true that they view emotions as distracting and unnecessary. They deal with problems by going back to their desk to work. This earth sign moon is practical and sensible, so a relationship's stability and longevity are more important than romance: the more dramatic expressions of love are not in their remit.

These moons are just as choosy in their friendships and prefer to mix with people of equal social standing, but once their friendship is given, it is forever—just like their love. Earth moons always play for keeps in every area of their lives. But party animals they are not, so don't be surprised if they sidestep any and all social invitations. In their eyes, a party offers no direct benefit, so it's wasted time when they could be at their desk, working. The exception is if someone of interest is also going to be there, someone who might help them in some way, or someone who could progress their career. Then they might just pop in for a while before slipping away.

Children are all part of their grand plan, otherwise what would be the point of all that effort? For Capricorn moons, life is about family. Once committed to someone, they have no intention of leaving. They are usually too busy working to stray, and anyway, they would find the whole business distasteful. So, a Capricorn moon chooses carefully; they take their time deciding.

This all sounds very worthy but a tad dull. And yes, Capricorn is often accused of that. Being ruled by Saturn does not help. All work and no play can result in depression or a spell of the doldrums. That's when their partners need to make sure Capricorn gets out for a day or goes on holiday. As a rule, Capricorn doesn't like spending their hard-earned cash, but if they do go on holiday, they prefer to go somewhere classy and stylish; they are rarely found at a crowded resort.

Capricorns only relax when they have reached a point in life they perceive as safe. Even so, they can only be who they are, so passionate encounters, emotional scenes, and dramatic confrontations are never going to happen. If people want a secure, stable life with a reliable, hardworking partner, they could do a lot worse than a Capricorn moon, because all the world's gold will they eventually lay at their partner's feet.

AQUARIUS MOON

Air/Water Combination

Positive Traits: Emotionally fun, friendly, nonjudgmental, gives partners space

Negatives: Unreliable, changeable, unpredictable, emotionally cool, detached

Air signs, it has to be said, are not the world's most passionate people. And logic—their forte—is not exactly the way to a prospective partner's heart. Yet, that is the best Aquarius can do, being so cool and detached.

Friendship, they do. That is easy. From an early age, Aquarius moons make friends from all walks of life. Because they are nonjudgmental, they somehow or another manage to befriend the child no one else wants to play with for whatever reason. Fast forward fifteen years or so and this is exactly what they do with romantic partners: select those most likely to surprise the family. It is impossible to foresee what anyone ruled by unpredictable Uranus might do at any given time, but suffice to say, Aquarius will rock the boat. It's unlikely they'll know why they are driven to do this. Perhaps it is curiosity? Maybe it's that zany sense of humour that secretly enjoys watching the fallout from their actions?

But Aquarius doesn't stop at rocking the boat—they often marry an unusual partner too. Perhaps they also do this out of curiosity? Certainly, it is not love. Or rather, not the sort of love the majority of people experience—that overriding, passionate desire for another—because, as stated earlier, Aquarius is an air sign, and air signs don't get blinded by passion.

Yet, Aquarians do marry and actually make remarkably good partners because they let others be true to themselves. They do not try to change people, hem them in, or control them. On the contrary, they give mates plenty of space and room to breathe and to grow. Aquarius only shrugs when asked if they have any preference, whether for food or where to go on holiday, or if having another child should be considered. In return, they expect the same tolerance and mild acceptance.

In an ideal world this might happen, but generally it doesn't. Partners of Aquarians are more demanding, more emotional, and far more stressed than their laidback air sign partner, which alarms Aquarius. It is not so much that Aquarius is unfeeling; more so, they don't know how to handle someone who is emotional or demanding. They stand back, thinking, *Whoa, what's happening here?* And they won't say anything supportive because they'll have no idea what to say, nor will they give their long-suffering partner a hug because Aquarius probably doesn't realise they need one. Consequently, they get called unfeeling and unsympathetic—and maybe other, less kind names.

Eventually, the emotional upheaval will all die down, and Aquarius will breathe a sigh of relief, but it is true that when the going gets tough, they get going. Many an Aquarian will walk out, leaving their other half in the middle of chaos. Chaos is exactly the sort of thing they cannot deal with. It would be helpful if Aquarius moons hitched themselves to people who were extremely active, tolerant, and grounded, who could cope with everything *and* forgive them when they return after the drama has abated.

Getting Aquarius into a commitment in the first place will be interesting. Because they don't have any rules, it is hard for others to play by them—especially the unwritten ones. Aquarius never acts according to plan or like anyone else. Relationships tend to happen by accident rather than design. A friendship might just result in a kiss. The typical Aquarian response would be to wonder why this person kissed them, but they will enjoy the experience and might just want to repeat it. Before they know it, they are walking down the aisle. That's because they gave that shrug when asked. Aquarius is nothing if not open to change, so they view the inevitable as another interesting experiment, another curiosity to observe.

And this is how Aquarius moons live their emotional life. Normal rules do not apply. Not only did they throw out the rule book, they never had one in the first place, nor do they intend to ever have one. Aquarians think life is so much more fun when they're just winging it, which is pretty much how they live their entire existence. They figure that you win some, you lose some; either way, they don't give a fig.

There is something totally refreshing, charming, and appealing about someone so unbounded by convention, who allows others to be themselves and who tolerates much. Aquarius moons are bizarre at times, absolutely unpredictable and totally out of step with normal life, yet they have a quirky, crazy sense of humour. The world would be so much duller without them.

PISCES MOON

Water/Water Combination

Positive Traits: Emotionally empathic, understanding, kind, gentle, trusting

Negatives: Confused, dreamy, unreliable, untidy, likely to walk away from trouble

Pisces is a mutable water sign. What does that mean? Water, in an astrological sense, means emotions and feelings. Mutable means changeable and flexible. This means Pisces' emotions and feelings fluctuate all the time, creating confusion and conflicting needs within them. Sometimes they may feel like a heaving ocean, at others like a fast-flowing stream, then maybe a trickling brook or at rest in a calm pool. From one moment to the next, they don't know how they will feel, so how can others?

The symbol for Pisces is the fish. It shows two fish swimming in opposite directions, which accurately describes Pisces' ability to see both points of view—but this, in turn, makes them unable to make decisions. Pisceans are renowned for being muddleheaded, and we can see why. How can they possibly make a choice when every option seems feasible?

For the natural world (and us) to survive, water is essential. It makes life possible. Being in tune with this essential life-giving element means Pisces has a depth and clarity of vision more farseeing than any other sign. They are highly attuned to all unseen vibrations and energies, yet Pisces moons often struggle to put their feelings into words. When they can't define something to others, they are viewed as hopelessly sweet but confused, yet in truth they are more aligned to nature's rythmns than any other sign. Most people love Pisces for this dreamy quality, though they might despair at times, too!

Romantically, Pisces moons are easy prey. Being so kind, charitable, nonjudgmental, and accepting, they have no radar to block those who want to control them. In general, they do seek a stronger partner—one who can handle the difficulties of life with ease—thus, they may find themselves involved with someone who walks all over their tender hearts. Pisces may be gullible, but they are no fool. If they find themselves in a bad situation, they will simply retreat from the relationship, usually without saying a word. They cannot deal with direct confrontation.

Being so receptive, gentle, and understanding makes a Pisces moon a wonderful friend and partner. They will listen for hours to their partner's and children's woes, make them a soothing cup of tea, and nod sympathetically. More than that, they cannot do. Even that simple act of genuine kindness exhausts them. Water has no stamina; when it builds up under pressure, it simply flows in a different direction. That is how Pisces acts when overwhelmed: they retire to have a nap, or they head to the studio to release all their worries about those they love in a work of art or a musical score. Pisceans find it easier to express things in an art form than in words.

Because they are so vulnerable and open to pain, Pisces moons get hurt many a time. When this happens, they retreat to allow the cool waters of forgiveness to wash over them. Sometimes, they get so confused by their conflicting emotions that they get tetchy and snappy, which is when partners should give them space. If a Pisces moon is curt, that means it all got to be too much—and it doesn't take much to overwhelm and exhaust a Pisces moon. Even the simplest of tasks are sometimes beyond them because they can't keep their mind on one job for long, so they often start tasks but never complete them, which is why most live in an untidy house.

Despite being so empathic and kind, this is actually a cool sign, and although they will love with their whole heart and would rather die than have their beloved family suffer, a cut-off point is necessary for their emotional well-being. Otherwise, they can get paranoid and so confused that they imagine all sorts of weird and wonderful things, making it hard to distinguish real psychic impressions from the concerns and worries inside their own head.

They need a partner who will love and cherish them, but who is earthy and practical. It's likely their partner will choose them, not the other way around, because even that decision will be impossible to make. A strong partner who makes the decisions Pisces finds so hard—who plans and organises, who books holidays and so forth—will be gratefully appreciated by Pisces; they look for a partner who will actively take charge of their joint lives.

In return, no partner will be more receptive and gentle, more supportive and compassionate, than a Pisces moon. They really are one of the loveliest people, and at their very best, they bring peace and calm to those who are momentarily broken. Pisces are old souls who have seen it all a thousand times before, but they can only offer love. Very often, that is all that is needed.

three
RISING SIGNS

Our rising sign is set at our moment of birth. It is the astrological sign ascending on the eastern horizon at that exact moment, so it is referred to as either the *ascendant* or the *rising sign*. Older books may use the former term, but it is now more commonly called the rising sign. Your rising sign can be any of the twelve zodiac signs because our planet is constantly turning. In fact, the rising sign/ascendant changes every two hours, which is why it is crucial to know exact time of birth.

Look at your birth chart. Although there may be planets in the first house, many times there are not. In general, we are not drawn to areas of the chart that don't have a planet in them (sometimes referred to as *empty houses*)—

they hold no interest for us. However, the rising sign is different in this respect. We consciously use our rising sign as a mask even if there is no planet there.

Why do we need a mask? Because we all need a little mystery when we meet people for the first time. We don't want to immediately reveal our true selves to strangers. First, we must decide if we like them and if they can be trusted. Until we have made those decisions, we subconsciously display the attributes of our rising sign as a protective disguise. Basically, our rising sign is how we present ourselves to others; it is what we want them to see.

Everything we say and do is filtered through our rising sign. Think of it as a doorway through which we must pass each time we interact with someone. But everything that comes *to* us from the world also comes through that same doorway, so we judge others through that sign too. No matter what our sun and moon sign, the zodiac sign that is rising on the eastern horizon at our moment of birth colours our every thought and action. For example, those who have, say, a caring Cancer moon and a fun Gemini sun but have Aries rising will filter all their reactions and words through the cardinal fire sign of Aries. Thus, their first reaction to anything and everything will be an Aries response; fast, assertive, confrontational, maybe bossy but certainly quite sure they are in the right. Those who know this person will be aware that although their first reaction is assertive and sure, underneath they have a heart of gold (Cancer moon) and a fun-loving, friendly nature which adores joining groups, teaching and learning (Gemini sun).

Not all of the rising sign characteristics are adopted, either. While reading the following descriptions, work out which bits apply and which don't. In truth, everything comes down to the rest of the chart. If the chart is mostly calm and logical but Scorpio is rising, the individual won't suddenly become dramatic and emotionally passionate when they meet someone new, but they will certainly appear to be secretive, private, and watchful. A stubborn, steady Taurus rising will not make someone more cautious if they are a wild child, but by the time everything has been filtered through Taurus it will certainly be a more reasoned and sensible response than it might have otherwise been, because Taurus rising slows things down. They don't act spontaneously, which will balance the wilder elements of someone with both their sun and moon in, say, fire signs.

There is one exception. If our sun sign is the same as our rising sign, there will be nowhere to hide—there is no mask. People with the sun in the first house are who they are, and others are hit by their full personality from the start. The sun has to shine and will push to be noticed. Famous people often have this sun placement.

This chapter is not just about our own rising sign. It is about other people's, too. With the exception of people with the sun in the first house, everyone wears a mask, but when we are around those who know and love us—our family, partner, and some close friends—we are comfortable enough to reveal our true self. Watch how others act when they meet someone new; they act differently because they have assumed the characteristics of their rising sign. Just for fun, try and guess which mask they wear.

It has long been believed that people tend to fall in love with those who have their sun sign in our rising sign, and my many years as an astrologer has borne this out. For example, if your rising sign is Capricorn, a person who has their sun in Capricorn will instantly appeal; there will be an immediate and natural rapport between you. So, if looking for a partner, this is a good place to start.

A lot is being written about rising signs right now. Many theories abound that we look like our rising sign. To a certain extent this might be true, but it is often too vague a premise to accept as fact. Some people do have the famed Scorpio rising intensity of gaze, the round moon-like face of Cancer rising, and the clear eyes of Virgo rising, etc., but it is by no means a given because there may be a planet (or more than one planet) in the rising sign. More than likely, the strongest planet's energy will predispose the individual to look more like the astrological sign that planet rules. For example, Saturn rules Capricorn, and if Saturn is in the rising sign (the first house), that person will probably look like a Capricorn—wiry, slim, with a tough constitution and a determined manner—regardless of their actual rising sign. But by all means, have fun trying to decide whether your friends and family are "true to type," and if not, check their chart to see if there is a planet in their rising sign and if that influences their general appearance and manner.

The way we use our rising sign as our doorway—whether we allow ourselves to be bombarded by the world and everything in it, or whether we use our rising sign as it is meant to be used, as a filter relevant to our own personality—depends on how evolved we are, and on our life lessons. There are many books out there that delve deeper into this mystery, but for now, let's look at it each rising sign's basic pattern of response.

ARIES RISING

Positive Traits: Happy and active, always has a smile at the ready, loves a challenge

Negatives: Speaks and acts before thinking, is too hasty in their decision-making, argumentative and bossy

What They Most Dislike: Anyone who presents an opposite point of view to their own, having to look after someone who is ill, listening to someone who is depressed, those who move or think slowly

Aries is renowned for being energetic, intuitive, fast-acting, and impulsive. That's because it is a fire sign, and fire is hot and quickly takes hold. Everything has to be done *right now*. That old saying "Fools rush in where angels fear to tread" is often repeated in regard to this sign, but it's very pertinent. Air signs use their mind to think things through before taking action, but fire signs don't. If something sounds good, Aries goes right ahead and does it. And in their trusting, childlike, optimistic way, Aries is sure it will all work out just fine.

So, yes, those with an Aries rising are impetuous, and impulsive, and all those other adjectives, but are also approachable and friendly, direct and honest, and easy to converse with. Don't try and argue with them, though, because they enjoy a verbal battle! They also speak without forethought and say the first thing that pops into their head, which will usually be something about them—how they handled a situation or person, or how they dealt with a similar problem. But these types of remarks are always said with the friendliest, most helpful intentions. Aries doesn't mean anything in a bragging way; they simply can't help relating everything back to themselves.

This is because Aries is the first sign of the zodiac, so it is the child in astrological terms. Think how a child acts and you have a good idea of an Aries rising's characteristics. Children are innocent and naive. They are friendly. They get excited about going on adventures and trying new things. They don't have any deeper machinations going on below the surface, and they have no conception of danger, thus they take unwise risks. This is the outer persona of someone with Aries rising. This is how others see them, and it imbues their whole personality with the drive to get things done quickly. Aries risings talk fast, drive fast, and move quickly. They speak without thinking and act on impulse. If someone opens a door, Aries rising is always the first through. They can't help it, and they don't instend to be deliberately selfish—there is nothing unkind about them—but with all that fire it is hard, if not impossible, to hold back from movement.

Those with an Aries rising can come across to others as slightly aggressive. That's because they get really frustrated with slower people. As everyone is slower than Aries, that means a lot of irritation and frustration coming from them! They are also inclined to speak their mind, even if it does sound a bit confrontational. They are not above shouting out of the car window if someone has done something they perceive as dangerous or silly, or even at a driver who is not as fast as they would like. They approach every situation like their symbol, the ram—by barging straight into things rather than avoiding confrontation.

And they rarely, if ever, compromise with others, so no amount of placatory talk will make them back down.

Aries is also a cardinal sign. This gives them a double dose of energy and drive because cardinal signs are proactive and courageous. With all this vivacity and enthusiasm, they don't allow anything to stand in their way or thwart them from their intended path. Wise words are ignored. And Aries don't really care if projects are destined to fail; they want to have a go anyway. Aries risings are full of confident optimism and feel sure whatever they do will turn out fine. Nothing fazes them. So, they won't listen to others who advise caution—often this will only arouse their anger. They absolutely hate when people give unsolicited advice or tell them to be careful.

Aries is the initiator. They start new projects and businesses and form new groups. They begin things. Totally bored by details, they soon lose interest in things that were exciting not long ago, but they're the perfect person to get the ball rolling! So, yes, an Aries rising may seem selfish to other, more sensitive souls, but they are simply being their irrepressible self and doing what comes naturally: being the child of the zodiac.

When Aries risings are around people they know well, their bossy, argumentative side will have a bit more rein, and they will become frustrated if anyone questions their plans. They like to have their own way and don't like postponing things to fit in with others.

Sympathy and compromise are two words this rising sign finds hard. They always have an opinion and never shrink from verbalising it, so they lock horns with those who argue back. And it is a fact of life that if anyone needs a shoulder to cry on, Aries is not that shoulder. They are doers: their astrological purpose is to initiate things, so playing nursemaid to someone who is ill is of no interest, and when it comes to emotional stuff, they avoid it like the plague. So, yes, people may accuse Aries rising of insensitivity, but they would be the first to agree! They really cannot be bothered with emotions—theirs or others'. Their motto is that an active mind and body is the cure to all ills, and who's to say they haven't got a point?

At a party or event, Aries risings have no problem entering a room full of people they don't know. Conversation comes easily—sometimes too easily! It is rare to find a quiet Aries. They will approach a stranger and say hi, and with their friendly, cheerful, chatty manner, they are incredibly easy to talk to. However, the conversation will be mostly about them: what they are doing, who they know, their future plans. Their sentences will be liberally scattered with personal pronouns.

With family, Aries risings can be brusque and blunt, especially if asked to help out more with tasks that don't appeal. They like to act independently, so they will expect partners to do the boring stuff in the household (or they will employ someone else to do it). Instead of doing dishes or laundry, Aries risings like to be out in the world, doing whatever it is they enjoy most. Yet, when left to cope, they are capable of making sure everyone is well fed, clean, and occupied—they just have little patience for moaners and the sick.

No matter what sun or moon sign people have, if Aries is rising, this is how they will appear to others, and how they will initially act and react to each and every situation and person.

Ways to spot an Aries rising:

- A friendly approach
- A lot of cheerful conversation about new project ideas
- Talking about themselves and their own plans before asking others how they are
- Making a future date/planning a meeting before the current event has even ended
- Handing out their phone number, or giving out their business card for further contact, to anyone and everyone
- Irritation if thwarted

- Rushing through an open door first or being first in a queue
- A sporty look, with a forward-leaning stance

As long as others don't ask anything of them and allow them to do whatever they want, Aries risings are the nicest, friendliest people you are likely to meet.

TAURUS RISING

Positive Traits: Reliable, trustworthy and true, are often good cooks

Negative Traits: Stubborn, slow, lazy, insensitive

What They Most Dislike: Having to put themselves out for anyone

Taurus is a fixed earth sign, and its symbol is the bull. That gives a pretty good idea of how people perceive them on first meeting. Fixed earth sounds pretty immovable, doesn't it? And as for a bull, well, have you ever tried to shift one when it was determined to stay put? Most of us are wary of even approaching one—we already know it will do exactly as it wants no matter what we say or do, and the last thing we want is for it to get annoyed—because that prospect is scary. Those with Taurus as their rising sign come across as stubborn, like that bull, and fixed in everything they do. That's because they know what they are doing and where they are going, and they are not swayed by whims and fancies or any other fleeting fashion.

Certainly, they are never moved off course by what other people think they should do. This makes them difficult to deal with, so they often come across to others as stubborn and cautious and, to the faster signs, frustratingly slow and unwilling to change or adapt to new ideas.

Taurus's aim is to build security. To that end they work incredibly hard, and they are more than happy to roll up their sleeves and do demanding physical work—to be honest, most Taureans prefer it to sitting in an office. All earth signs like the outdoors, and Taureans, being strong characters, are not fazed by a bit of wind, rain, or even snow and ice. They are capable and calm, and they exude an aura of reliability in every situation.

Yes, they can sit out at night under the stars and gaze in wonder at the complexity of the universe like the rest of us, only they don't spend their time wondering why we are here and where we might go when we die, not unless they have a more intuitive sun or moon. Taurus is fixed in the here and now and attends to the practical details of life. Their mindset is: Why worry about what you cannot know, or cannot change? Sounds pretty sensible, and Taurus is nothing if not sensible. That doesn't mean they can't be moved by a sweet song, a soft sheet, a naked body, or a delicious meal (all of which they adore), but to truly impact a Taurus, the approach has to include something they can touch or smell or use. For this reason, esoteric subjects are of little interest to them.

It's lovely to know that in this unpredictable world, Taurus is always there. Through thick and thin, through the ups and downs of life, through illnesses and traumas, they will still be beside their partner in old age, solid and reliable as a rock in a stormy sea. Whether it is a friend, partner, or family member, Taurus never lets down someone in need—as long as it is practical help that's required. (For emotional support, it's best to turn to Cancer or Pisces.) If someone wants help building a house, decorating, or sorting out the garden, or if they're just looking for somewhere to stay for a while, Taurus is the sign to call.

A Taurus rising will do what they can to help, even if they haven't seen someone for years. If a distant friend or family member turns up at their home complete with suitcase, Taurus will invite them in without the faintest look of surprise or a murmur of complaint, and they won't even mention that it's been thirty years since they last saw each other. No matter how much time has passed, Taurus won't look much different. They weather well. Maybe it's that calm demeanour and unruffled manner, but they manage to look almost as good as they did all those years ago, although their waistline may have expanded. (Taurus adores food.) And once they've agreed to help someone in need, Taurus will whip up a delicious and sustaining meal (see!). In the presence of a Taurus rising, guests will feel themselves relaxing and letting go of all their pent-up tension. It's as if they've come home to Mum or Dad; Taureans are so supportive, assured, and capable. Without rushing or seeming to hurry in the least, the bed will be made up, the meal prepared, and a bottle of wine provided. Guests will be wondering why they've let so long pass since they were in touch.

If someone is looking for a lively, interesting, full-of-variety life, it has to be said, Taurus rising is not for them. Taurus risings don't say much—they don't even do much—but they are *there*. Always. Rarely do they lose their temper, but if they do, beware. Why would you deliberately anger a bull? Just remember this sign is fixed earth and change is anathema to them, so don't even think to suggest it.

No matter what their sun and moon sign, when everything is filtered through the steady, calm, implacable sign of Taurus, these people do nothing hastily. Any impulsive act will be tempered and calmed.

Who else but Taurus would still be living in the same house thirty years on? They seek stability and security, and they would rather have no mortgage and savings in the bank, so often stay put even when they can afford something bigger and better. Taking out loans and maxing out credit cards is not their style in any shape or form. Taurus prefers to stay put in the same place/town, preferably the one in which they were born, and cannot see the point of foreign travel when their own backyard is so beautiful. They don't like places that are too unfamiliar, and they will never attempt to learn another language. Heavens, a typical Taurus rising hardly speaks much anyway, so why would they need to know even more words?

Even if a Taurus rising has a Gemini or Sagittarius sun or moon (the two signs *least* likely to want stability), if they make a commitment, they make a commitment. If they say they will do something, they will. Those with Taurus rising work incredibly hard to build lasting structures with secure foundations, and their love life is no different. Once given, their love is forever, so its best people don't mess them about or play games. If a breakup occurs, Taurus will recover because they are strong. The loser will be the one who left: what they thought was a dull-looking stone just happened to be a diamond.

People who know Taurus risings see them as being stuck in their ways and unwilling to compromise. It annoys them when Taurus refuses to conform to what they want. Eventually, friends might stop inviting them along to activities because they usually say no. Taurus risings are often perceived as lazy, too, because they never rush around. If something is too much trouble, they simply won't put themselves out to do it: this stubborn sign won't compromise for anyone. Despite that, once they start moving, they do achieve a huge amount of work because of their inner and outer strength. Their placid, steady demeanour is restful, and people often seek out Taurus risings when life has been unkind because they are soothed by Taurus's calming presence.

The family of a Taurus rising will love them and despair of them at the same time. Taurus cooks fabulous meals and is always there for them, but they groan at the way Taurus lets good opportunities pass by because they simply cannot be bothered to make that extra bit of effort.

Ways to spot a Taurus rising:

- Comes across as calm and reliable, no matter how anxious/unsure they feel inside
- Steady demeanour; always there for people when they need help
- Takes things slowly; never rushes
- A salt-of-the-earth friend who will never let anyone down
- When they fall in love, it is forever
- Once a plan is formed, they find it really hard (if not impossible) to change tack

- Has a hard time adapting to new ideas and suggestions because they prefer to do things as they've always been done
- Incredibly stubborn
- Isn't interested in doing fun things just for the sake of it because everything has to have a purpose and a result
- With the bull as their symbol, they often have a sturdy, substantial look

Despite all this, Taurus risings are adored because they are so trustworthy and capable.

GEMINI RISING

Positive Traits: Finds joy in everything, witty sense of humour, loves life

Negative Traits: Unreliable, changeable, doesn't turn up when they say they will, changes their mind from one moment to the next

What They Most Dislike: People who are dull, boring, and overly emotional

Geminis live in the here and now. Forget the past, never mind the future—for them, it is what is happening *right now* that is exciting. Whether it's celebrity gossip and intrigue, news of the rich and famous, reality television, or the latest advances in science, art, media, or information technology, they adore it all.

Regardless of their sun and moon sign, those with Gemini risings are likely to be the first in the queue for the newest mobile phone or computer because they love communication and travel in each and every form. That's because Gemini is a modern version of Hermes, the Greek god who relayed messages between the other gods of Olympus, and as the best way to pass on information is the latest way, it's easy to see why Gemini risings are fascinated with just about anything that makes communicating faster and more exiting.

But those with this rising sign are not limited to a fascination with communication. They are curious about everything and anything. They have logical, questioning, and naturally curious minds, but because they have so many interests it is impossible for them to delve into one in great depth. They wouldn't want to, anyway. They are experts at skimming the surface, excellent at selecting the most relevant and pertinent information (so they can sound knowledgeable on any subject) and then moving on. Because of this, they rarely identify with any particular point of view; they are not interested enough to develop a view of their own. Gemini risings are best at adapting their opinions to blend in with those around them in a chameleon-like way; they say what people want to hear.

Other people's ideas and opinions fascinate them, but as far as Geminis are concerned, arguing a point is a complete waste of time. A day or two after a conversation, others are likely to hear their Gemini rising friend or partner repeating what was said to someone else. This is perfect, because their role is to pass on information.

Gemini likes to be where it's at; they like to be in the know. Their idea of hell is to be stuck in the same job with the same people doing the same thing every day for, seemingly, forever. There is a whole world out there just waiting to be discovered and they want to be part of it—and how can they do their astrological job if they never meet anyone new or go anywhere? Is it any wonder they get panicky when they feel trapped? Restrictions and boredom bring out the not-so-nice aspects of their character, but if they have freedom to move around and move on, no one is a more delightfully funny (and fun!) companion than a Gemini rising.

Gemini's symbol is the twins, which accurately describes their dual nature. Most of them have more than one job at a time, or they split their day between two different activities. Certainly, they will have lots of jobs during their working life. It's common for Geminis to have at least two marriages. It is as if they need one for each twin! Without a doubt, they can rapidly move from one twin to the other, being either the charmingly witty side of their personality or the caustic, snappy, irritable one, depending on the circumstances.

Because they are not emotional and not at all earthy, Gemini risings like to keep relationships light. Even with a more earthy sun or moon, it will be quite hard for them to maintain long-term partnerships because of this change-ability and desire for variety. Security is at the bottom of Gemini's list of priorities, and friendship and having fun are at the top, so the repetitive aspects of daily life are not easy for them to handle. A relationship that requires any sort of commitment is a challenge, but they might be lucky and find a tolerant and understanding partner who allows them to come and go as they please.

Gemini rising's unreliability is a big problem for others to wrap their heads around. It's frustrating when Gemini turns up late. Their apparent disregard for inconveniencing others is most annoying, but it never crosses a Gemini rising's mind that other people might actually care if they appear or not, or that that they might have planned their day around being with them. Guilt is not an emotion they feel, so if others make a fuss they will be bemused at best, and irritated at worst. Too much of a fuss and Gemini rising will make a quick exit. So, yes, they lack reliability and staying power, but they make up for it with their love of life. No one is more fun to be with. No one has wittier one-liners than Gemini. No one else is so bright and breezy and fun to be around. So, it's hard for people to stay annoyed with them for long.

Gemini's constant interest in people and life itself gives them a youthful quality that keeps them mentally active with the passing years. They live lightly and do not drain those around them. On the contrary, they bring lightness and joy whenever they pass by. Family members and close friends who know and love Gemini risings don't expect them to take sides or be dependable.

Ways to spot a Gemini rising:

- Constantly changes their opinions
- Always agrees with everyone to keep conversation flowing, light, and friendly
- Loves to hear what other people think
- Is charming and fun with a witty, sometimes sarcastic sense of humour
- So clever with words that others can't help but laugh
- Friendly with everyone, but hard to pin down to a time and place; usually late for meetings or fails to even turn up
- The go-to person for up-to-date news and advice
- Easy to get on with and rarely argues, so they can diffuse tense situations with a joke

- They have bright eyes and quick minds and are usually slim

Geminis are who they are and cannot pretend to care about deep issues. When people get emotional and needy they look for an escape route, so others should learn not to ask much of a Gemini rising.

CANCER RISING

Positive Traits: Genuinely loves others, compassionately understands others' suffering, willing to do what it takes to make others feel secure

Negative Traits: Overly sensitive to the point that people feel they are walking on eggshells, bursts into tears a lot, moody, overprotective

What They Most Dislike: Cruel words and unfeeling people

Cancer is a water sign ruled by the moon. This produces an ultrasensitive and very emotional person. No matter what their sun and moon sign are, those with a Cancer rising will present as a person easily roused to tears, who can be moody and changeable and difficult to understand because of their fluctuating inner feelings, but who is caring and thoughtful.

Cancer risings are not afraid to show empathy for others. For the unemotional, detached signs, this can be a real

turnoff, but they won't care. They like being compassionate and caring toward others; they like being a good lis-
tener; they like being a genuinely lovely person who offers
sympathy and understanding when other people are in
crisis or are suffering. They really care about others—or
at least that's what they portray with this rising sign. They
seem receptive and perceptive to others, so even if they
have a tough sun and moon, they will come across as sympathetic and understanding, willing to be anyone's shoulder to cry on. Having this rising sign bestows empathy on
even the hardest of hearts!

Cancerians know that when people are at their low-
est ebb in life it is important to be able to talk about their
problems with someone who can relate to them. Being
an empathic water sign, Cancer allows people to sob and
moan and complain that life isn't fair, and they do this
without telling them to get a life (fire signs), that things
will sort themselves out in due time (earth signs), or hastily leaving the room (air signs). With a Cancer rising, others know they can open their hearts and that their secrets
are safe. A Cancer friend/partner/family member offers
empathy, compassion, and a genuine desire to help.

The reason Cancer rising is able to provide respite
for others is because they understand pain and how horrible it is to suffer. Despite appearing strong and capable
on the surface, underneath they are extremely vulnerable,

which is why their symbol is the crab. Their soft underbelly is what makes them so receptive to pain: they are finely attuned to unkind words and actions from others. When people are cruel (whether real or imagined), Cancerians are shocked and deeply hurt, especially when they do so much for others.

Those with a Cancer rising seek emotional security. They require a safe haven from the pain in the world. Their oasis in an unfeeling world is usually their partner, close family, and their home, where they can retreat to lick their wounds when life has been particularly cruel. But they always emerge again, because Cancer is a cardinal sign and has the strength to rise from setbacks and face the world. They can hold down a demanding job *and* continue to be caring and kind, but each little barb knocks another small chink from their armour.

The number one priority for Cancer risings is finding a partner. That takes some doing for such a sensitive sign. Who has never been hurt in the search for love? Most of us get over things and move on, but it is not so easy for Cancer. Each time a prospective partner lets them down, all the past disappointments resurface, and they despair of ever finding someone who really cares. Because they have an idealised view of the past, Cancers always believe people were so much nicer in days gone by—more considerate, more loyal, more trustworthy. But because the driving force of Cancer's life is finding the perfect partner, creating the perfect family, living in the perfect home, and making sure their children have a perfect childhood, they keep striving to bring their dreams to reality, so out they go to face an unfeeling world. No matter what their sun and moon sign, those with Cancer rising need an emotional aspect to their lives, to be caring and kind and to help in whatever way they can.

Once Cancer rising takes the plunge and commits heart and soul to a partner, it opens a whole new can of worms. Their protective nature ensures feeling pain on their partner's behalf, and they die a hundred deaths for their children when they struggle through the trials of childhood. A Cancer rising would willingly take all the pain on themselves to spare their beloved family. Their way of protecting others is by creating a home that is a haven. Most Cancer risings adore cooking and are adept at making their house a home that is cosy and warm, and they work at jobs that provide emotional nurturing too. They know how to surround not only their loved ones but those they meet every day with the emotional security they so desperately need.

People with a Cancer rising are hardworking and caring and want to live a life that is meaningful; they need to feel they've done some good, helped someone, been of use to others. Without an empathic aspect to their life, things feel empty and meaningless. That's why people with the sign of Cancer in their chart are often carers in some capacity; they simply must express their genuine concern for the welfare of others.

A Cancer rising likes nothing better than huge family gatherings. While people eat and laugh, they will stop a moment and gaze at the result of all their efforts and a warm glow of satisfaction will fill them from head to toe. This is what Cancer does it all for: moments of love with extended family all enjoying being together.

With people they know well, Cancer risings allow their emotions full rein. They are self-sacrificing, adoring, and tender—yet emotionally demanding and temperamental. With family, Cancer risings can freely show their insecurities and moodiness, but their abiding love for family is obvious, so family members tolerate their fluctuating feelings.

Ways to spot a Cancer rising:

- A caring and kind manner; empathetic
- Provides a sympathetic ear to anyone who is struggling
- Receptive to people
- Cries easily
- Appears moody and changeable
- Is often misunderstood, but is understanding and supportive when others need help
- Seeks a life that helps their fellow man

- Often have the look of the moon: a round, full, soft face

Cancer risings are understanding and sympathetic when others are going through hard times, though maybe a bit overprotective. Because they are moody and easily upset, people often feel they are walking on eggshells, and those who are more practical and logical will feel exasperated and annoyed by the emotionalism Cancerians display. But those who have been at the receiving end of their compassion and understand greatly value someone who really does care.

LEO RISING

Positive Traits: Willing to put their life on the line for those in need, capable of any sacrifice, commanding, loyal

Negative Traits: Needs constant praise and appreciation, wants to be the centre of attention

What They Most Dislike: People not saying thanks for what they do

Leo's symbol is the lion, the king of the jungle, and Leos are nothing if not regal in manner. So, those with a Leo rising will have a certain something in the way they present themselves, an innate self-confidence and style. Coupled with their disarming charm and charismatic, assured confidence, they naturally inspire respect from others. No matter what their sun and moon sign—and even if they don't feel confident inside—Leo risings appear as if they have life sussed. They are never afraid to stand up and give a speech, or to be the spokesperson; they will always step forward.

Leo rising are friendly, active, good-tempered, and extremely capable, and they're not at all worried if the buck stops with them—they can handle it. To be truthful, they prefer it. Being centre stage and the focus of everyone's attention is their driving force, and they are astrologically designed to take charge. Look around and you'll see Leos everywhere: at the yacht club organising the next regatta, at the community centre making a list of who is doing what at the next fair, at the hospital arranging for the dignitary's visit, or at the church planning for the visit of the bishop. Everywhere, there are Leos making sure an ordinary event becomes a special occasion. Of course, not all of them will shine on a big stage, but they need to feel important and be recognised for their input, even if they achieve this by being number one in their family.

People with Leo rising get things done. And they do it with such good humour and cheerfulness it is hard not to get swept up in their enthusiasm. With their charming and persuasive style, Leo believes challenges are there to be met and overcome. They can turn their hand to almost anything; their outward manner opens all sorts of doors. Their job in life is to express the qualities of the sun, their ruler, which is why Leo risings are irrepressible. Even a less-bold Leo rising will have a quiet confidence and the ability to shoulder responsibility. Indeed, they may even look for opportunities to express their protective nature. But even quiet Leo risings want to be appreciated for their work, just as bolder Leos do.

Which brings us to their Achilles' heel: the need for praise. Leo rising can, and will, expend any amount of energy and effort on behalf of others, but woe betide if they are not given a vote of thanks for it.

They can be bossy and stubborn, and because Leo is a fixed sign, they will never back down or apologise for anything. Can you imagine a lion apologising to his cubs? Instead, Leo risings will stalk away when upset, but inside they will be crying. They did so much and no one appreciated them. Nothing is a sorrier sight than a sad or disappointed Leo.

With this rising sign life is a stage, and Leo is in the spotlight. Yet they are not all show and no substance. They really do know how to get things done, they really do know the right people to approach, and they really are brave, courageous, loyal, and loving. Their activities are not just for self-aggrandisement, but to help those less fortunate, those less talented or secure: children; the old, ill, or infirm; anyone and everyone who needs a strong and loving hand to provide for their needs. It is Leo's hand that will be extended in true and genuine concern. They show by example. But they are human, and they will expect thanks—better yet, praise! Praise a Leo and they will glow with inner pride, then move even more mountains on behalf of others. Their warmth and loyalty are a beacon. And a word of thanks is hardly difficult when they do so much.

With family, Leo risings can be bossy, but they are ultimately caring and warm. They give lots of hugs and exude charm and style, but they still expect constant recognition and praise for all they do. Ideally, family members look up to Leo and adore them, because this is necessary for their self-esteem. Leos need to be number one in their partnership as well, and if a partner fails to appreciate all that Leo does for them, Leo sags with despondency and then seeks out someone who *will* put them on a pedestal.

Ways to spot a Leo rising:

- A warm, friendly, commanding manner
- Confidence in the way they hold themselves
- Proud but stubborn
- A ready smile, a willingness to help, an enthusiastic charm

- The ability to organise others in a way that does not create resentment
- Expects, and adores, thanks (preferably praise) for all they do
- Someone saying they look good raises their spirits
- Can get quite upset if people ignore them
- Usually they walk tall and have a proud, commanding manner. Not all stand out, yet there is still a quiet confidence about them. Many have the look of their symbol, the lion, having a mane of reddish hair. They are always noticed when they enter a room, and what they wear and how they look is really important to them

Leo risings are warm and encouraging, unafraid of embracing challenges in life.

VIRGO RISING

Positive Traits: Hardworking, self-sacrificing, kind

Negative Traits: Fussy, nitpicky, a moaner

What They Most Dislike: Untidy, uncouth people who don't care how much mess they make

Virgo is ruled by Mercury, the planet of communication, and in this mutable earth sign, the result is someone who has great clarity of vision—not in the spiritual sense, but literally. Every speck of dust, every fault, every failing, and every negative trait are as clear as day to those with a Virgo rising. Virgo's symbol is the earth maiden who enjoys doing practical tasks, so they feel an inner satisfaction when they organise and arrange and everything is perfect. They enjoy looking after people and being of use, but they see all the things that need to be done so clearly that it often feels overwhelming.

That's because the world is a disorganised place. People are untidy. Faults are to be found everywhere. We are not machines, after all, and Earth is a place of chaos, so how can Virgo tidy everything up? The answer is they can't, of course, but they will do their level best.

It must be very hard to see work everywhere, to want to put everything in tidy compartments. It must be horrible to be aware of the great disorder of life and know that creating change is an impossible task for one lone soul. But they aren't alone, of course. There are millions of people out there with at least one planet in Virgo, all trying to sort things out. And thank heavens for them, because those of us without Virgo placements rush through life leaving unfinished business. What would we do without someone efficient and organised, someone who not only notices what needs to be done, but dutifully does it? The whole world would surely grind to a halt if it wasn't for Virgos everywhere, cleaning up other people's mess.

Yet, the harder Virgo rising works to eliminate disorder and replace it with a workable system, the more they despair. They see the monumental and hopeless task it is, but still they try. Is it any wonder they can get sharply critical, or that they tend to worry and fret and fuss? Life is one big, never-ending tidy-up job.

So why do they bother? Because Virgo rising feels threatened by disorder. They devote time to keeping their mind tidy, their clothes neat, their world organised: their house, children, and career will all be efficiently compartmentalised. Virgo always knows exactly where anything is at any given moment, and they often don't need a to-do list because their head holds all the details of what needs doing. Household chores, house repairs, car servicing, insurance details—Virgo recalls it all.

No matter what sun and moon signs they have, those with Virgo rising are perfectionists with impossibly high standards. While they might manage to live up to their own expectations, the rest of us fail miserably, which is why people with Virgo placements are renowned for being nit-picky and critical of their friends, partners, and children. This isn't done with ill intentions; Virgos are simply trying to make everyone as perfect as they are! But people don't like to be criticised; their egos are fragile enough without having someone moan about the mess they are making as they go about their daily lives. While Virgo risings wonder why everyone can't tidy up after themselves and save them having to do it, the fact is, most people aren't even *aware* of the jobs that Virgo thinks need doing.

Even if Virgo rising has an otherworldly Pisces or Aquarian sun or moon (two signs renowned for being nonjudgmental), this rising sign will most certainly judge! They can't help it; they see everything so clearly it is hard to ignore someone's dirty coat or smudged mascara or askew tie. When they walk in a room, they will always notice a stain on the carpet or the frayed edge of a cushion. And wonky pictures drive them nuts. They simply won't be able to resist going to straighten it. Even worse for them is someone munching loudly on an apple, or a repetative sqeak from someone's shoe!

As a rule, Virgo risings don't like showing their emotions and can appear calm and unruffled in all circumstances— but they won't be able to resist pointing out these faults. If someone argues back, their in-control mask may slip a little. Being attacked or criticised themselves throws Virgos off guard. This is because they're always doubting their own capabilities, and they see their own faults more clearly than anyone else does anyway, so this shakes their confidence.

Virgo risings come across as organised, dutiful, and kind, willing to do anything, from making tea to editing the president's speech. They are grounded, sensible, and efficient. On the surface, Virgo risings are selfless people who would never shirk a duty, no matter how inconvenient. They do what needs to be done without expecting thanks or praise. This sign is also renowned for its earthy sexiness, but like everything else about Virgo, they keep that firmly under wraps. They don't share their feelings until they are sure they will be reciprocated.

People know they can rely on a Virgo rising because they never let anyone down if they can help it, and they are rarely late. Always ready and willing to help out at any event, the local community will benefit from Virgo's kindness and charity. Virgos are good and trustworthy friends. Family members adore Virgo risings because they do so much for them, but they can get fed up with Virgo's constant complaining that they have to do all the work. However, it's true, and family members know it.

Ways to spot a Virgo rising:

- A kind, dutiful, modest, helpful person who willingly rolls up their sleeves to help out
- Organised and practical with an eye for detail, but also critical and hard to please
- Judgmental of other people who are less tidy, clean, or organised

- Sees everything, even the smallest speck of dust; nothing gets past their super-observant gaze, which is why they are so good at detailed tasks
- Self-sacrificing; they try to please others by being adaptable
- They often have large, clear eyes and a critical, watchful manner—suffice to say they are always spotlessly and neatly dressed!

Others appreciate all Virgo does for them and the sacrifices they make, though they sometimes feel Virgo worries too much about the small stuff.

LIBRA RISING

Positive Traits: Lovely manner and delightful smile, willing to listen to everyone, has a logical take on all situations

Negative Traits: Doesn't allow people into their life unless they can come up with the goods in terms of money or lifestyle

What They Most Dislike: Dirty, rough people who have no charm or saving grace

The first thing people notice about Libra risings is how lovely they are. Not only is this sign renowned for being good-looking, they are also charming, courteous, and balanced. That is what they are like half the time, anyway.

Libra is the sign of the scales, which aptly describes their up-and-down energy levels: everything has to be finely tuned to balance properly. So, Libra will be heavenly most of the time, but when the scales dip, they may feel lazy and bored. No matter what their sun and moon sign, Libra risings appear cool, calm, balanced, and reasonable half the time, and for the other half, lazy and uninterested in anything. However, because they are ruled by Venus, the planet of love, they will always be charming and courteous. Even when feeling grumpy, Libra risings can't bring themselves to be rude or confrontational, and they still manage to look gorgeous even at their worst.

Libra risings thrive on friendly cooperation and compromise, and even those with a more aggressive sun or moon sign will mellow remarkably when filtered through the sign of Libra. Because bad feelings upset them, they strive to bring peace and harmony to all situations. They rarely argue; they discuss. Libra is always willing to listen to someone else's point of view. They adore extended conversations when they can present the opposite view— as long as no one loses their temper and the discussion stays logical and objective. They steer clear of emotionally charged discussions and will either change the subject or leave the room, because they believe strong emotions cloud judgment. They are right, of course!

Libra's ability to see every point of view is great until partners want them to take their side. It will be annoying when their Libra rising partner stays so calm and logical, especially when their partner feels really affronted. Having the opposite point of view pointed out to them is not what they want! But Libra's dulcet voice, gentle demeanour, and reasonable logic remind others there is not much they can do but calm down and accept that Libra does have a point. Libra is ruled by the scales for a reason; their astrological purpose is to bring arguing factions into harmony. Libra risings seek justice and fairness, which makes them sit on the fence in all situations. So, when friends or partners are angry with someone, Libra won't be able to take their side. Instead, they will act as a mediator. That is the role they excel at and the one they were designed for, and Libra's greatest gift to the world is their nonjudgmental acceptance of everyone's point of view. They are an air sign, after all, and they use their mind to make decisions, not their feelings.

While Libras may be nonjudgmental when dealing with everyone's *point of view*, they are not at all easygoing about their surroundings. This is the sign renowned for liking and needing the best in life, so not only are they very discerning in their friendships and partnerships, they expect their home to be—at the very least—comfortable and clean, but ideally, it will be luxurious.

It's impossible for them to find harmony and peace when exposed to the rougher elements of life, so Libra risings use their considerable intellect to make enough money to distance themselves from the rowdy crowd. They are quite happy to marry for money, too. The further away Libra is from gritty reality, the happier they feel. But wherever they live, their home will be the peaceful, classy haven they so require, and to be accepted into their life, friends and partners needs to be a class act—they won't mix with just anyone.

Libras spend their lives trying to keep the scales in balance, but they are rarely in balance themselves. Half the time, they get up at six for a run before work; the other half, they're unable to get out of bed in the morning. Either way, it is almost impossible to get annoyed with them. Venus flashes that oh-so-innocent and heavenly smile and the wind is instantly taken out of other people's sails. When the planet of love decides to use its charm, there is no chance of resisting!

People love being around Libra risings because of their gentle manner and personal beauty. Family members know Libra risings keep the peace, so they run to them when there is an argument; others know Libra will always find a solution that everyone can accept. They appreciate the lovely surroundings Libra has created, but they have learnt not to expect too much, especially when Libra is in one of their lazy periods.

There is no doubt anyone with Libra in their chart knows just how to host a classy party or event; nothing will be overlooked. But maybe guests should head home early, because Libra always makes good use of those who offer help—if guests stay around too long, they may be the ones cleaning up the mess at the end of the night while Libra relaxes on the sofa in apparent exhaustion!

Ways to spot a Libra rising:

- A calm, balanced demeanour
- Willing to listen to people's opinions and provide a sensible, balancing argument
- Rarely outwardly flustered
- Always logical
- Selective of their friends
- Sports a visible designer name
- Great at delegating, especially the menial tasks
- Always looks classy and stylish, even after exercising!
- Are usually attractive, with a dimple or two and a delightfully charming manner

Libra risings are the first person others ask for advice if they are facing a dilemma. But remember, they are better at mental tasks than physical ones; those they happily delegate!

SCORPIO RISING

Positive Traits: Totally loyal, deeply passionate, will
   never betray or let down a loved one

Negative Traits: Secretive, controlling, watchful

What They Most Dislike: People finding out who they
   really are

The sign of Scorpio has a reputation, and it is not unfounded. Scorpio is a water sign and, as such, they are deeply emotional. But this puzzles others, because Scorpio always looks so calm and in control. In fact, they don't even look as if anything is bothering them! Scorpio stares out from a calm mask with their intense eyes, listening, watching, waiting, and analysing. And the reason they look so calm is because they dare not show their true feelings. Scorpio never, ever reveals anything; it is far too exposing to have their feelings spread out in the open. All their weaknesses and vulnerabilities out there for others to see? No way! People might take advantage. The sign of Scorpio would never do anything as rash as that. That's why they are often accused of being secretive. They don't know why they like to keep themselves private, they just do. Their deepest fears and dreams will always remain hidden, even from those they love.

Even if they have no personal planets in this sign, a Scorpio rising acts in a true-to-sign manner by only showing people what they want them to see, selectively hiding bits behind a veneer of capability and strength. This is unique behaviour: *Scorpio hides itself even when it is just a mask.* In other words, most people use their rising sign's characteristics as a form of protection, but Scorpio, being so secretive, even enjoys making this "mask" elusive. So, spotting a Scorpio rising is not an easy task. Maybe look for the person who gives the least away!

The first thing others will notice are their eyes. Scorpio rising's eyes are always very intense, no matter what colour they are, and will seem to bore right into others. It is almost as if they can read their minds. And guess what? They pretty much can. Because Scorpio is a deeply intuitive sign, they are highly attuned to nuances. Scorpio is never interested in the superficial, but wants to get to the very root of everything, and that will include anyone they meet or anything they undertake.

Because Scorpio risings have this uncanny ability to instantly sum up people, they make a decision about someone as soon as they meet. But even if they accept someone as a friend or lover, Scorpio will always be watching and waiting to make sure they are indeed loyal, and they will dump others without a second thought if they are betrayed in word or deed. Second chances are never given. To a Scorpio rising, total loyalty is nonnegotiable.

They will appear calm and in control, but Scorpio rising is always watching from inside the mask, sussing out who people really are and what they want. Because they are naturally suspicious and assume everyone wants something from them, they are rarely scammed; they spot a conman a mile away, and they wonder why their more gullible friends and family cannot see what is, to them, so obvious!

So, they keep others at arm's length—even best friends, partners, and family, despite loving them deeply. There is always a barrier, no matter how thin the veneer, between a Scorpio rising and others, and this is regardless of their sun and moon signs. Even a cheerful, trusting Aries sun will be more watchful and cautious with this rising sign.

Being allowed to fully know them is probably never going to happen. Various people will be given glimpses, but no one will be allowed complete access; that would make them vulnerable, and no way will they ever allow that. Scorpio must have control, not others. Friends and partners may think they have them sussed, but a Scorpio rising will never allow a person to know them inside and out. They always have secrets.

This may sound frustrating, but others find this quality intriguing. There is something bewitching about those intense eyes. And because Scorpios are interested in eso-teric subjects and the beyond, entering into a friendship or relationship with a Scorpio means a lifetime of discovery. There are no guarantees people will ever truly understand the Scorpio rising in their life, but it's worth it. No one gives more of themselves than a Scorpio, which sounds like a contradiction, but it isn't. They give 100 percent of their energy and time, but never the entirety of themselves. They enjoy being the gatekeeper of their own secrets.

Life is never a superficial affair for Scorpios. If people prove themselves loyal, Scorpio rising will defend them to the hilt; if family, to the death. With friends, Scorpios are a little less guarded, but no one will really know them. Scorpios show what they want others to see and keep their deeper feelings hidden. In return, Scorpio risings are good and loyal friends, willing to do almost anything if asked, but absolutely fixed in their stubborn determination to be true to themselves and their own ideals. They will never make compromises and are never swayed by others, even those they deeply love. No one can make them do any-thing they feel is wrong, or do anything they don't want to do.

Family is incredibly important to a Scorpio; this is the closest they get to revealing their true self. Family mem-bers know Scorpio will put their life on the line for them. In return, Scorpios expect to be able to trust their family completely and are absolutely devastated if anyone betrays them. As an enemy, Scorpios are implacably cold. They never give people a second chance.

Ways to spot a Scorpio rising:

- A calm, in-control facade
- Appears as if nothing bothers them, and that they don't care if they win or lose (boy, do they care!)
- An implacable stubbornness
- The desire to keep their own secrets
- Never flashy or obvious in their dress or manner
- Their manner suggests they do not need, and certainly don't want, advice
- Watchful and assessing; they rarely, if ever, get conned
- A subtle sexuality
- Many have an intense and penetrating gaze

Even if a person's only Scorpio placement is their rising sign, others should be aware of the sting in the scorpion's tail. When Scorpio goes cold toward you, you'd better back off—quick.

SAGITTARIUS RISING

Positive Traits: Friendly, warm, willing to have a go at anything

Negative Traits: Unreliable, changeable, hard to pin down in every respect

What They Most Dislike: Clingy, emotional people and being trapped

Sagittarians are busy people. This is a fire sign, and all fire signs are active with lots of energy, but Sagittarius is also a mutable sign, which means they are changeable and flexible. This combination of fire and random energy produces someone always on the go, always busy, very friendly, but with scattered energy.

Those with a Sagittarius rising never say no to suggestions because they are impulsive, inquisitive, and afraid of missing something. Always saying yes means they are destined to experience a multitude of different situations throughout their life. Life will be a parade, a colourful affair full of activity and fun, friendship, and travel.

Because of their innate cleverness, they gather intuitive information wherever they go, then freely dispense it to others in the form of wisdom. But unlike Gemini (who also gathers information), there is nothing superficial about Sagittarius rising. They may seem superficial at times because of their scattered interests, but this couldn't be further from the truth. In fact, all Sagittarians seek answers to the big questions and are fascinated by foreign cultures, languages, ancient civilisations, esoteric subjects, and just about anything that may enlighten them as to humanity's purpose here on Earth. With this rising sign, absolutely everything they see, do, and hear is filtered and analysed to see if it promises to hold the "truth" of our existence.

It is this search for the truth that makes them so restless. It isn't always a conscious search, but at some point, as they move from place to place and person to person, they feel sure that one day life will make sense. Sagittarius risings love learning new things, especially when it involves subjects that stretch their inquisitive imaginations. Their eyes positively light up when someone imparts new and interesting information.

The problem is, usually Sagittarius is so busy travelling, talking, seeking, learning, and exploring, they miss special moments. And even when they are present, half their attention is on their next adventure. This applies to the people around them too. So involved are they with their own projects, they frequently overlook the signs that loved ones need them.

Like all fire signs, they are impetuous, driven, and fast to act. Because this sign is mutable (meaning flexible), their drive is unfocused and random, which is well described by their symbol, the archer. The archer shoots his arrows, and where they land, Sagittarius rising goes. If the archer sent out only one arrow, no problem! But the archer sends out at least half a dozen, which aptly describes how many projects this rising sign has on the go at any given time. Sagittarians rapidly move from one project to the other, often leaving jobs half done, abandoning projects halfway through, and discarding ideas when something more exciting or interesting comes along. That is not to say they are halfhearted about anything they do. Their enthusiasm is unbounded, but they may (or may not) get around to a project or person again—it all depends on if something, or someone, else turns up. Hence, they are prone to unreliability.

Like all fire signs, there is a tendency to be rash. Sagittarius risings don't sit and consider things first, they just do them. Some things will work out and some won't. Either way, they are not concerned, because they have a million other ideas just waiting for their attention. This rising sign makes multitasking look like child's play! They always do more than two things at the same time.

There comes a point when those who know them wonder just what it is they are rushing around looking for, but Sagittarians are so warm, friendly, affectionate, and easygoing that others can't help but like them. Friends will be able to cope with the way Sagittarians pop in and out of their lives; their Sagittarius friend is such fun, always suggesting places to go and things to do. But when it comes to love, partners are going to have to be incredibly tolerant. Loved ones have to accept that their Sagittarian partner needs friendships and to have long conversations that may stretch into the night, but usually there will be no need of jealousy. In fact, by complaining, partners may just push Sagittarius rising into an affair, even when it wasn't even on their mind. This rising sign won't accept any restraints at all!

Downsides? Of course there are. Not only do Sagittarians seek the truth, they speak it. Renowned as the bluntest of the astrological signs, Sagittarius risings are unfazed by stating the unvarnished truth, and it takes a thick hide not be hurt by their words. It is wise to never ask them for an opinion unless you are able to take the answer straight on the chin. Sometimes blunt to the point of rudeness, they never prevaricate when it comes to honesty. "You asked, didn't you?" will be Sagittarius's response if someone takes umbrage. They have no intention of being unkind—they just say it how it is. The truth is important to them.

Sagittarians need personal freedom, and they will not allow others to control or curtail them. Sagittarius rising are as impossible to catch as flying embers from a fire. They scatter their energy far and wide in numerous projects, a myriad of friends, and as many adventures as can be crammed into a lifetime. Spontaneous and a risk-taker, they love nothing more than a gamble. It might not be a literal bet; they enjoy taking a chance on something or someone. Jupiter, their ruling planet, is considered lucky, and this imbues them with an innate belief that they will always land on their feet. Mostly, they do.

Family members know Sagittarians are hard to pin down and need the freedom to come and go. Sagittarius adores when loved ones gift them interesting esoteric books or hands-on courses instead of presents, and a partner would be wise to keep the excitement alive by suggesting intriguing holidays and random days out. Sagittarians are warm and affectionate partners and parents, but they abhor details and must feel free.

Ways to spot a Sagittarius rising:

- A happy, friendly, busy persona
- Loves adventure and excitement
- Always willing to have a go at most things, even with a jammed schedule
- Their door is always open
- They have friends from all walks of life
- Jealousy and suspicion pushes them away
- They must be free, or at least feel they are
- They radiate energy, enthusiasm, and happiness, and are usually dark haired

Sagittarius's numerous friends accept them for who they are: a fun person who is not always reliable because of the hectic nature of their life.

CAPRICORN RISING

Positive Traits: Reliable, strong character, determined to succeed

Negative Traits: Workaholic, not generous, prefers routine and safety

What They Most Dislike: Shallow or unreliable people, as well as wasting time and money

Those with a Capricorn rising come across to others as extremely serious and worthy. And, because this rising sign is often dedicated to keeping fit, they can seem quite severe in look and manner. There is an austerity about them, an earnestness, that gives the impression that others are playing at life while their Capricorn rising friend/partner is actually doing it properly. And there is no question that they do see life as serious business; Capricorn believes they have a job to do and that anything worthwhile takes a long time—life is too precious to waste on frivolities.

This rising sign gives the phrase *self-discipline* a whole new meaning. Ruled by that stern teacher, Saturn, they can take care of themselves very well, in every sense. Like their symbol, the goat, their aim is the highest pinnacle of success so that they can look down from on high. No obstacles or difficulties thwart a Capricorn rising from their path. They are in no hurry, so they are quite happy to bide their time. Capricorns are perfectly sure that dedicated hard work and determination will pay off in the end. And it usually does.

Like all earth signs, Capricorn risings want to achieve something worthwhile and tangible. To be of value it must be real; there must be visible proof, like their body being honed and fit. Their bank account, too, will be pretty fit for purpose if true to type. Concrete evidence of the success of their efforts is necessary, preferably in status and wealth. What about praise? That's all well and good, and everyone likes to be admired now and then, but it doesn't put money in the bank or food on the table, does it?

Regardless of their sun or moon sign, Capricorn risings enjoy presenting this stable, reliable, safe persona, and they like nothing better than when others ask for their advice. When Capricorns give advice, it will be wise, sensible, and trustworthy, albeit safe. A Capricorn rising does not take risks, or if they do, none that would jeopardise their status or wealth.

There is always pleasure to be found in achieving a hard-earned goal, but this sign rarely allows themselves time to enjoy their well-deserved reward. When one task is completed, another is set. It's no wonder that they can appear a bit pessimistic, dour, and cautious. Letting their hair down is not something a Capricorn rising knows how to do, unless they have more sociable sun and moon positions. Social events are generally not of any interest, and dancing on tables after too much alcohol is never going to happen! Because family is important to them, they will attend big events in life—christenings, marriages, funerals—but usually leave after a suitable amount of time. Making small talk is not their thing.

While fire signs are impulsively rushing through life, scattering their energies far and wide, this cardinal earth sign slowly builds their future. It isn't just for them, but for the generations who come after. Capricorns undertake the long game. Tradition is extremely important, as is family. They see themselves as just one cog in the family line, and because they are not selfish or impulsive or vain, they don't mind if it's their great-grandchildren who get all the accolades. They just want to play their part in building familial security, and real security has nothing to do with celebrity status or get-rich-quick schemes; it's about longevity, tradition, conservatism, and being someone in the commercial world. The phrase "old money" is so Capricornian, it was probably invented by one!

Capricorn's shoulders are immense. People in need know they can turn to them, not for emotional advice or intellectual insights, but for real, solid, practical help. As long as this rising sign is sure others will use their advice sensibly, they will help as much as they can. But if the person seeking help is unreliable or untrustworthy, Capricorn won't waste the time of day on them—and that applies to their romantic partners, too.

Whether with friends or strangers, Capricorn risings behave exactly the same. They are who they are and have no need of artifice. They willingly give their time and energy to the worthy, but they won't waste time on shallow people. And because they are focused on building wealth, they rarely give loans, but they will do so if they sense the person asking will use the money wisely—and perhaps increase it.

Family members know Capricorn risings are 100 percent reliable and trustworthy. They will work long hours and make huge sacrifices to make sure their loved ones are safe, secure, and comfortable. Sure, Capricorn risings aren't going to set the world on fire with their enthusiasm, but family members admire their courageous staying power as well as their determination to be the best in their profession.

Whatever their career choice, Capricorn risings aim to succeed, no matter how long it takes. Capricorns become judges, hold important roles in financial institutions, or go into politics—they do the serious jobs. With their great strength of character, dedication to the path they have chosen, and tremendous ability, it is no wonder Capricorn risings find the places most suitable for their talents—and their talents are considerable. Whatever pinnacle they end up standing on, they have assuredly earned it.

Ways to spot a Capricorn rising:

- A serious, mature manner
- The ability to give wise advice
- A no-nonsense approach
- Dependable and reliable
- A love of family and tradition; is pleased when family members do well in life
- Keeps fit into old age (this rising sign is renowned for looking younger with each passing year)
- They have a wiry, slim, yet strong body and deep-set eyes

In truth, others are bit in awe of Capricorn's inner strength and of what they have managed to achieve in life.

AQUARIUS RISING

Positive Traits: Drifts through life without getting upset about things, has an open door to anyone in need, clever and original mind, mild demeanour

Negative Traits: Doesn't notice when people need them, doesn't want to get involved, not tactile

What They Most Dislike: Emotions, demanding people, and being trapped

It is very difficult to write about a typical Aquarian because there is no such thing; it is an enigmatic sign. This unique energy can be seen in its ruling planet, Uranus, as well. Technically, Uranus is a gas giant, and therefore it is not actually made of rock (except for a small inner core). Uranus's many moons are described by physicists as random and unstable because of their conflicting gravitational fields, which make their orbits unpredictable. Because Uranus rules Aquarius, this is a sign renowned for sudden breakthroughs, transformation, and change—and unreliability, eccentricity, and originality.

Aquarius is an air sign, but it is a fixed sign too. How can air be both unpredictable and fixed? Isn't that confusing? Therein lies the difficulty when attempting to explain what Aquarians are like! Think of a swirling wind sweeping along a sidewalk, blowing leaves in all directions. This is how those with an Aquarius rising act and think. It is impossible to catch them; just as others think they have them in their grasp, they swirl away. The fixity of the sign means Aquarians have a stubborn streak, and in this case, it means they are absolutely determined to be themselves. Aquarians will not allow others to change them or hem them in. They are determined to blow whichever way they please.

Suffice to say, Aquarius risings cannot be pinned down. The only thing that stops them from running completely wild is that most of them have a negative self-image. Either that, or they don't think much about themselves at all. Their minds are on a different plane altogether, so whether they look good or not is often of no consequence. That's why most of them dress unusually. They just adore off-beat fashion. Their bizarre appearance might be because of their desire to shock (Uranus), or perhaps they just hadn't actually noticed what day it was, let alone what clothes they put on that morning.

It is obvious, then, that the first and easiest way to judge who has an Aquarius rising is to pick the person wearing the most unusual outfit. There will always be that stand-out *something* that declares an Aquarian. Because our world is more tolerant than it used to be, it is not as easy to shock or surprise others, but those with an Aquarius rising will still find a way. They like doing the opposite of everyone else. They enjoy being different. Aquarius risings do all the normal things in life, but in a slightly different way.

Life is simply a curious phenomenom to Aquarians. No matter what their sun and moon signs, Aquarius risings appear detached, cool, and unpredictable, with the need to do things differently from everyone else. They consciously choose not to get personally involved, preferring to watch life as it unfolds like some sort of circus parade. They stand on the sidelines and figuratively scratch their heads, thinking, *Why do people act this way, or do that? What is the purpose of all this random behaviour?*

Because Aquarius risings need to analyse and assess, everything they do—and everything that comes to them—is first viewed through the lens of unpredictable Uranus. How can this be made more fun, more interesting, more unusual, more amusing, more *anything* other than same old, same old? Aquarius rising takes information and figures out how to shock with it and how to bend it to new uses; they endeavour to see it from a different angle. That's why they are renowned for breakthroughs in science and electronics, physics, math, and medicine; any subject where new ideas and theories are sought, you are sure to find Aquarius suns, moons, and rising signs.

Despite having a detached view of the world, Aquarius risings will probably do what everyone else does: marry and have children. Why? Because that, too, is a curiosity. There is nothing more intriguing to an Aquarian than love. They may just commit to someone to find out what all the fuss is about. Life is one big question (or rather, a series of questions) to an Aquarius rising. Even so, they are free spirits and never take anything personally, not even love—and this applies regardless of the sun and moon signs. Those with Aquarius rising will keep a certain coolness and aloofness in their outward manner, and they will seek someone just a little bit different.

The day-in-day-out routine of life is not their scene at all, so it's best they find someone organised and sensible who can attend to the practicalities. It's also worth noting that Aquarius risings are not overtly passionate or tactile; most actively dislike demonstrative displays of love. A squeeze of the hand is fine, and a quick hug might be tolerated, but they find floods of tears or outright drama absolutely terrifying. Rather than providing comfort, they are more likely to open their eyes wide in shock and then quit the scene. Getting an Aquarius rising involved in an emotive discussion or expecting emotional support from them is a road to nowhere. If you lean into them, you will fall over.

Occasionally, Aquarians might simply disappear—usually when their partner is particularly in need. Dreamy, otherworldly Aquarius risings probably haven't noticed their partner is stressed, or if they do, it doesn't fully register that it has anything to do with them. If the drama is too chaotic and noisy, they are likely to just walk out to find some peace. Without a shred of guilt, they go, leaving their long-suffering partner to cope. They might head out for a run or a cycle ride, to meet a friend, or to go for a drive; there was just an overwhelming need to flee. But Aquarius invariably comes back, because no fixed sign likes change for the sake of it, so partners need to be not only capable, but also forgiving!

While Aquarius rising will happily work at any job, they are better suited for an environment that leaves them free to wander in and out. Most people with Aquarius placements are night owls for some reason, so they prefer heading to their desk when a sudden, unexpected, and out-of-this-world idea occurs to them. (For this, we have Uranus to thank—again.) Failing that, a job where they can work unsupervised would be good. They may not stick to regular hours, but because their sign is fixed, they will always finish any task they have started.

Ambitious they are not (unless they have a sun or moon in Capricorn, when they will be ambitious but choose a slightly different job or way to achieve their aims). Generally, worldly success is not something most Aquarius think much about. That's because they live somewhere in the realms of space, mentally speaking. Somehow, though, most of them manage to live well even though they lack the slightest interest in finances or material things.

Friends accept Aquarius's quirky nature and admire their ability to be nonjudgmental and accepting 100 percent of the time. However, they have also learnt that their Aquarius friend isn't emotional, so they won't share their problems or ask for advice. In times of turmoil, Aquarius's calm, unperturbed manner is soothing.

Family comes to realise Aquarians love in a detached way. Loved ones see Aquarius as unemotional and unreliable, but they appreciate that although Aquarius dances to a different tune, they do care for others in their own unique way.

Ways to spot an Aquarius rising:

- A friendly, nonjudgmental manner
- A willingness to accept people from all walks of life
- An open door for anyone who needs a place to sleep, without expecting thanks or any return at all
- Gives people space to be themselves
- Likes to shock others by saying, doing, or wearing something unusual
- Always presents as calm and relaxed
- Cannot be relied upon
- Easy to spot because they like to shock, so there will be something unusual about them, plus they have a relaxed, easygoing manner

Aquarius risings accept everyone—high or low, rich or poor—and make no judgments. We are all just curiosities to them.

PISCES RISING

Positive Traits: Understanding and compassionate nature, loves everyone unconditionally

Negative Traits: Disappears when things get tough, unable to focus for long, untidy, forgetful, vague

What They Most Dislike: Deadlines and aggressive, angry people who shout or demand things from others

Pisces is the twelfth sign of the zodiac, the last and final sign. Because of this, some say that this mutable water sign encompasses parts of all the other astrological signs. But Pisces hasn't any similarities to Virgo, Taurus, or Scorpio, or even Aries, to name but four. Pisceans are kind, gentle, compassionate, and nonjudgmental, and none of the other signs combine all these delightful characteristics into one bundle of genuine sweetness.

With no effort at all, they absorb nuances, vibrations, and auras from wherever they happen to be. Pisces risings won't notice the carpets or wallpaper in other people's houses, but they will definitely know if they are in a happy home because they easily sense underlying tensions. That's because Pisces is a water sign. All three of the water signs are emotional and sensitive, but Pisces is also mutable, which means shifting and changeable. This sign represents ever-flowing, moving water, and that is how Pisceans live and think: in this dreamy, watery, feeling place without roots or ambition, drifting wherever the tides take them, ebbing in and out according to their mood.

So, yes, a Pisces rising does come across as dreamy and vague. Certainly, they are not logical. They do have feelings, although not necessarily *emotional* feelings. Pisceans tend to have intuitive feelings. Because they are so busy picking up the vibes of a place, they often miss the details, so they may appear bumbling and hopeless to the logical signs. But non-verbal messages are clearer to Pisces than words; words just cloud the issue. After all, people lie, don't they? People say what they think you want to hear. They pretend they are fine when maybe they aren't. So what use are words? And what is the point of facts and figures when they can be so easily manipulated into what others want them to be? Anyway, Pisceans understand everything by just sitting quietly and tuning in.

Okay, so this approach isn't going to get Pisceans high up on the ladder to success in material terms, but they don't care. It's hard for them to handle anything that calls for organisation, detail, and schedules anyway. And Pisceans think success, fame, and fortune are like everything else: an illusion that people hide behind. People are not simply a job or a bank balance. Pisces sees behind the facade, but anything they glean will be kept to themselves unless others ask for advice. And Pisceans never make any judgments because they accept life as it is, with all its joys and sorrows, the good and the bad. Pisces risings feels the whole of life: they are, after all, part of that river that is ebbing and flowing, moving unceasingly from its source. Is it any wonder they lose their bearings sometimes? They have no compass except their intuition; they accept everybody and everything and believe there are no rules except compassion and love.

This rising sign makes for a genuinely lovely person. They work willingly for and with those who are less fortunate, give of themselves as a matter of course without thinking of personal reward, and listen unceasingly to people's complaints and problems—all the while asking for nothing in return. Naturally, they get tired, weary, and upset by things—and usually more quickly than the rest of us, because of their deep understanding. Preventing themselves from becoming too personally involved in the lives of others is a difficult task for one so sensitive and understanding, yet Pisces risings instinctively know when to retreat for their own sanity. They cannot take all the world and its problems on their shoulders, no matter how much they wish to.

Because they are so receptive and understanding, the pain of humankind is sometimes too overwhelming. For self-preservation, Pisces risings will slip away to recover and restore their own balance. Most likely, they will head toward water, their natural element. Failing that, Pisceans may also be drawn to the forest, where they can be soothed by nature. Many Pisceans are artistic in some way and find solace in expressing their inner selves in a work of art or through music.

Friends know Pisceans are people they can unburden themselves to who will not tell them to pull themselves together. They are totally sympathetic, understanding listeners and very kind people. But they cannot cope with stressful situations, and they will always seek a way out. Emotional confrontations (as well as business ones) are actively avoided. Pisceans always take the line of least resistance and never confront situations.

Family members adore a Pisces rising's sweetness and kindness but despair of their inability to focus on details. They know they will be loved and listened to, but the house may be a bit disorganised, messy even. Ambition is not a strong point for Pisceans, but family members are so deeply loved and cared for that they forgive Pisces's vagueness and inability to give them the material comforts of life. Family members know that when Pisces starts irritably snapping at them, they are in need of some quiet time on their own.

Ways to spot a Pisces rising:

- A gentle, sweet, compassionate persona
- Easily tired and easily hurt
- Willing to do anything for others if they can manage it
- Often disappears without warning

- Doesn't turn up for work if too much is dumped on them
- Has a creative streak
- Always the first person everyone goes to when troubled
- Has a very kindly demeanour and appears quite shy

Pisceans are rightly referred to as old souls. They know the meaning of true acceptance, of nonjudgmental love and compassion, and this is the gift they bring to others.

four
SUN AND MOON SIGN COMBINATIONS

Combining two signs is a bit like cooking: some ingredients work better together than others! This is especially true for the sun and moon because they are such powerful planets. The following descriptions are a summary of how the sun and moon work in real life when their energies are combined. Remember, the sun embodies our outer persona and the moon relates to our inner emotions, but sometimes we have suns and moons that are so different we have difficulties reconciling our life drive (sun) and our emotional needs (moon).

Rising signs are not included in this section because they are an astrological sign, not a personal planet like the sun and moon.

ARIES SUN/MOON COMBINATIONS

Aries, being a cardinal fire sign, is no pussycat! Remember, Aries is full of drive and energy. They're fast acting, and always without much prior thought. Having a water moon will provide them with more empathy, an earth moon will ground them, and an air moon will bestow some necessary logic, but Aries is an independent, won't-be-told-no sign, and that will always shine through.

ARIES SUN/ARIES MOON

Wow, with this combustible fire-fire combination, there will be no stopping this firebrand. A person with an Aries sun and moon will embody impulsive, impatient action. Most likely, they will have a risky career or a dangerous sport as a hobby to enable them to live life on the edge. They are very independent and won't be told no; partners will have to be very tolerant and understanding and expect little attention. Their best partner may be an earth sign who is happy to stay home and who allows Aries to run wild or, alternatively, a cool Aquarian who won't mind at all when Aries heads out without warning. Emotionally warm but not empathic, they don't wallow in emotions and will hate it if their partner does.

ARIES SUN/TAURUS MOON

The Taurus moon will calm some of the Aries impetuousness, thus allowing for stable partnerships. This is quite a nice balance. Aries has that warm, affectionate nature and Taurus is all about sensuality. This combination will make this person quite tactile. They might be lacking in compassion and finer feelings, though, which can be a bit tough on partners. They need someone who is a balance of energy and stability, just like them. Practical and sensible, they want to build something lasting. With that being said, they will still demand their independence now and then, even though they can be a bit possessive of their partners. In other words, they expect complete autonomy over their own life but rarely allow partners the same freedoms. A bit bossy and stubborn, but they look after mates well.

ARIES SUN/GEMINI MOON

Busy, busy, busy! It will be hard to pin down this whizz kid. They're full of ideas, have loads of friends, and can talk the hind leg off a donkey. They're cheerful, light, optimistic, and full of bonhomie. They are clever with words and always coming up with new schemes, most of which are not thought out. As a partner, they are often unreliable. When they get an exciting new idea, they have to head off to put it into practise right then and there, so partners need to be steady and tolerant and sort out the basics of life.

ARIES SUN/CANCER MOON

This is a lovely balance of cheerful empathy. Cancer will understand and offer sympathy, and Aries is always willing to help, so this is a kind, energetic person who is a good homemaker and parent. They are perfectly capable of coping with the demands of both home and work life. Both signs are cardinal, so they can quickly recover from any disaster. Cancer provides emotional security and Aries lends its drive and optimism. Aries will feel the call of freedom now and then, but they will rarely leave a relationship if there are children involved or if they have a dependent partner.

ARIES SUN/LEO MOON

This pairing of two fire signs makes for a charismatic, chatty, colourful person who likes being the centre of attention. They have very little interest in sensitive matters, but they're kind and protective if given enough praise for their efforts, which will be considerable. They are full of energy and joie de vivre, but they will head off when things get too emotionally demanding. Security issues may be a problem area as they are not given to thinking about stability. However, the Leo moon is fixed, so they will prefer to stay put in relationships as long as their partner also loves to dress up and party and doesn't forget to praise them.

ARIES SUN/VIRGO MOON

This is a very decent person who is both energetic and has an eye for detail, so they are someone who works hard on behalf of others and does the necessary jobs without expecting praise, although a word of thanks now and then would be appreciated. They will expend all their energy on doing jobs, both at work and at home. They rarely relax because their Virgo moon sees all the tasks that need to be done, and their Aries sun has the energy and drive to do them! But they can get irritable and fretful if they feel too trapped, as Aries sun needs a bit of personal freedom. They would benefit from a more relaxed partner who would encourage them to chill and who gives them some personal space now and then, well away from chores.

ARIES SUN/LIBRA MOON

These two opposite signs work well together. Aries does not usually compromise, but with a Libra moon they will be pleasant, agreeable, and able to make concessions. This is a good mix of energy and intellectual logic. Libra hates arguments, so this moon placement will calm some of Aries's more aggressive aspects, and the fire of Aries will give Libra some necessary get-up-and-go energy. This is a good working pairing that gives the possibility of career success, while home will be a place to restore their energy before heading out into the world again. They will want a house that is spacious and beautifully furnished, and appearances will be important. Partners may have to provide the emotional support to family as neither sign is renowned for being particularly sympathetic.

ARIES SUN/SCORPIO MOON

This is a difficult person to manage because they must have control and be in charge in all aspects of their lives. Aries is normally chatty, but Scorpio will hold back on giving out too much information. So they have an energetic, cheerful outer persona with a deeply emotional moon that watches for trouble. Quite a combination to handle in relationships. Very independent and uncompromising, yet passionate and driven. Partners will have to be tolerant and able to withstand Scorpio's possessiveness while allowing them to live as they please. They absolutely know they are right and won't be told anything, so they're easily annoyed if anyone interferes.

ARIES SUN/SAGITTARIUS MOON

A wild-child persona. Neither of these fire signs are able to be tied or restrained in any way, so this person must be free to follow their own independent route in life. They are impetuous, impulsive, and unpredictable, with scattered energies and lots of things on the go at any one time. They have a huge number of friends, and they always forget to phone home, so a very tolerant, patient partner will be required to handle this combination. They're a risk-taker, and they will be averse to commitment in any way. They are unlikely to manage long-term relationships unless Venus or Mars is in an earth sign.

ARIES SUN/CAPRICORN MOON

A great pairing of fire and earth gives them great staying power and drive to achieve their highest aims in life. They are going places! They are a good relationship prospect who will make sure energy goes into creating tangible security; they seek status. They aren't interested in emotional drama, and this combination isn't sensitive in any way. A good, practical, hardworking family person, ideally matched with a water sign to bring some balance into the mix and provide emotional support for any children.

ARIES SUN/AQUARIUS MOON

This is someone who will be friends with everyone. A lovely, uncomplicated, and relaxed person who seems to manage life just fine, but who does not make a good partner as they are not interested in security, nor are they in any way compassionate; they will walk away when anyone gets too upset because they can't handle it. They're more interested in being friends and having a good time, though they may commit in a weak moment. And, as Aquarius is fixed, they may stay if given enough personal freedom by a patient partner. Sometimes they act a bit off-the-wall when that Aquarius moon appears, so they may say or do unexpected—and even outrageous—things.

ARIES SUN/PISCES MOON

This is a very sweet person under a more aggressive outer shell. Both signs are kind, though Pisces is more deeply compassionate and caring. Both like to help, so others will be given their full attention and time, but they find it almost impossible to sustain this supportive energy as they are easily tired and get bored of ongoing drama. Neither sign has their eye on finances or security, so they would work best with a more earthy partner who can give them some stability. Intuition is their forte, but they lack logic and often rush into things before thinking. They act solely on their instincts.

TAURUS SUN/MOON COMBINATIONS

Taurus is a fixed earth sign, so having a different moon can actually be beneficial, as it will lift their stubborn implacability a little. Fire moons will give them more drive, air moons will make them more detached and less possessive, and water moons will give them a greater depth of emotional empathy. Earth moons will emphasise their earthy traits.

TAURUS SUN/ARIES MOON

Aries will give a much-needed boost of energy to Taurus, creating a lovely combination of friendliness and reliability. This person is totally trusting and trustworthy. They're not very emotional, but they are warm and sensuous. They have less staying power in relationships than most Taureans, but they're also more adventurous. They are quite stubborn, opinionated, and emotionally tough, but they genuinely seek the best outcome in everything they undertake, romantic or otherwise. They are easily misled and deceived by others, so be kind to this honest soul.

TAURUS SUN/TAURUS MOON

Stubborn, fixed, determined, and earthy, what you see is what you get with this combination. They are a totally reliable, dependable, stable person who will work extremely hard to create safety and security for their loved ones and themselves. However, they will resist change of any sort. They're not adventurous or interested in an exciting life. In fact, they're happiest at home by the fire, having a nice meal with family. They're prone to putting on weight because of this lifestyle, and because they are disinterested in action, they are hard to motivate. They cannot see the point of extending energy without a tangible result. Instead, they would rather relax and enjoy themselves. They love all the pleasures of the flesh.

TAURUS SUN/GEMINI MOON

Gemini's lightness of mind will lift Taurus and make them lighter and freer, more accepting of change and variety, while the fixed earth quality of Taurus grounds Gemini. This is a complex mix of stability and instability, of reliability and unreliability, of the butterfly personality of Gemini with the fixed stubbornness of the bull. Taurus sun will still want security, but Gemini moon will be very sociable and enjoy learning new information. This person will converse easily, but at the same time, they'll be ready to go home. Neither sign is emotional, and neither like dramatic scenes or angry encounters. They make friends easily but keep them for years. This person is more talkative than most Taureans.

TAURUS SUN/CANCER MOON

This person is totally devoted to family. A Cancer moon brings a nice emotional and caring quality to the earthiness of Taurus. Family is incredibly important to both these signs, so they will build an amazingly loving and secure wall around their loved ones. Losing a family member (through any means) is devastating to them. If a partner walks out, they will never forget and never forgive, feeling hurt forever and finding it hard to trust again. Moody and silent at times, they are a thoroughly decent and caring person who is willing to do whatever it takes to look after those they care for.

TAURUS SUN/LEO MOON

This person is going places! Leo seeks the limelight, and Taurus provides the necessary staying power to reach the dizzy heights of fame. Both luxury-loving, Leo will delight in being noticed, and Taurus will enjoy the money and security—plus the access to luxury hotels and fine wining and dining. Both are fixed signs and don't like change, so they will stay with their partner for life as long as their partner provides lots of earthy sensuousness and heaps on plenty of praise. They are destined to be rich or, at the very least, very comfortable financially.

TAURUS SUN/VIRGO MOON

Both the sun and moon are in earth signs, so this is a very sexy, sensual, and grounded person. Both signs seek stability, but Virgo is a little more flexible (although Virgos are inclined to focus so much on the details that they may miss the overall picture). They are a good and reliable partner who can tolerate the ups and downs of relationships. Overall, they are dutiful and kind, albeit a bit of a stick-in-the-mud. Totally trustworthy and stable, they are a good homemaker, even though they may be a bit nitpicky and critical at times. They tend to get bogged down in duties and work, so they need an active partner who will drag them outside for a hike or something similar.

TAURUS SUN/LIBRA MOON

These people are after the very best in life. Both signs enjoy luxury; Taurus prefers the earthy, sensual pleasures like eating, drinking, and making love, and Libra the calm, luxurious atmosphere of grand hotels and places that distance them from the harsher realities of life. Although Libra moon will happily marry for money, both signs are capable of working hard. Taurus is not afraid of hands-on hard work, and Libra is intellectually astute. Combined, this sun and moon make a formidable team. They will be loyal to a mate who looks the part and supplies the indulgences.

TAURUS SUN/SCORPIO MOON

This combination brings together the earthy sexiness of Taurus and the scorching intensity of Scorpio's passion to create someone for whom the physical expression of love assumes top priority. Incredibly possessive, inclined to jealousy, and amazingly stubborn, they prefer to focus on one partner for life. They will never walk out on a partner unless pushed to the extreme limits of their endurance, which is considerable. They are implacably determined to live life on their terms, though, so the question is, can partners cope with not only taking second place, but the feeling of being under house arrest?

TAURUS SUN/SAGITTARIUS MOON

This person combines earthy stability with the need for emotional space, making this a hard partner to understand. They might create lots of security and then simply walk out one day. They're inclined to bluntly speak their mind, regardless of the consequences. They are a very complicated individual who will need a partner who understands that sometimes, despite their devotion to loved ones, they need to feel free now and then. Give them enough personal space and they might stay put, but partners will need to be tolerant, grounded, and loyal.

TAURUS SUN/CAPRICORN MOON

Both the sun and moon are in earth signs, so this will be a totally reliable person with an eye on security and stability. They play the long game. Their focus is all on money and status, so they may lack an adventurous spirit and come across as a bit staid. They have no time at all for wastrels or dreamers. It's easy for them to tread on other's sensibilities because they lack compassion and empathy, but they will stay with one partner for life if they can find someone who appreciates their efforts and doesn't expect an emotional response. They're very interested in comfort and sensual pleasures, but they will accrue more than enough money to indulge their every whim. They won't fall for just anyone; they seek someone classy and reliable.

TAURUS SUN/AQUARIUS MOON

This is a difficult combination. They have an earthy drive to be secure, but they also prefer to be emotionally free and independent, so they're a hard person to fathom. Both signs are fixed, so this is a stubborn person who is determined to live life the way they want. Partners will have to adapt—they certainly won't. Taurus sun will need security and safety and will focus on building a house and home, but Aquarius moon will provide a quirky inner nature that brings a breath of air to relationships, lightening the Taurean heaviness. Taurus likes the earthy pleasures, so partners will have all the necessities of life and plenty of cuddles, though neither sign is particularly sensitive or intuitive, so partners may feel misunderstood. A great deal of tolerance and adaptability will be required, especially when Aquarius moon does its thing and sets out to be different.

TAURUS SUN/PISCES MOON

This is a very reliable and sweet person who is stable and yet deeply compassionate. They will create a wonderful home for their family and supply endless sympathy, though they may be lacking get-up-and-go energy, as Taurus can be lazy at times and Pisces gets easily overwhelmed, so their house will be homely but untidy. They're a lovely person, but they are at their best when they have an active partner who can drag them out now and then and shake them out of their lethargy, as they can spend many an hour just sitting and dreaming.

GEMINI SUN/MOON COMBINATIONS

Geminis are changeable and unpredictable, so a moon that provides some grounding is useful. Earth moons calm them, fire moons spur them on to new adventures, another air moon will exacerbate their need for personal freedom, and water moons will give them some much-needed empathy and compassion for others.

GEMINI SUN/ARIES MOON

Aries moon brings warmth and physical energy while Gemini provides Aries with a less impulsive, logical view, so this combination works well together: it creates someone who is fast and light, fun and driven. However, there will be a lack of compassion for partners and a general distaste for overly emotional people and situations, so they will tend to avoid those with water moons (Cancer, Scorpio, and Pisces). Nor will they understand earth signs and their need for security. Both Aries and Gemini are busy signs, interested in the here and now and having fun, so are difficult to tie down. They are too independent and freedom-seeking to be interested in a long-term commitment, but they may stay in a relationship if enough excitement and variety is provided.

GEMINI SUN/TAURUS MOON

This creates a contradictory mix of wanting to feel personally free and yet needing emotional stability and security. This person might choose a partner who will stay home while they roam about in the world. They alternate between being cool and sensuous, so partners may find them changeable and unpredictable. They get an emotional fix from nature and the outdoors, but they must be up-to-date with what is going on in the world, so they can't live in a wild, remote place. They lack physical energy, so a fire sign partner could provide a good balance.

GEMINI SUN/GEMINI MOON

Light, cheerful, and incredibly clever with words, this person is the epitome of Peter Pan: always youthful, always on the move both mentally and physically. This double air sign uses words in life—not emotions—and will actively avoid confrontation or drama involving emotional matters. They're unlikely to be touchy-feely because such a free spirit is a true messenger of the gods, flitting here and there to talk. They have numerous interests and hundreds of friends because they are lighthearted, fun, and a great storyteller and joke maker. Ideal jobs for this person are writing comedy programmes, hosting talk shows, or being a salesperson extraordinaire—basically, working somewhere words can be used cleverly. They are unlikely to want to commit to anything forever, whether that's a career or a relationship.

GEMINI SUN/CANCER MOON

This is a complex mix of caring emotion and needing to be detached from the emotional and physical demands of others. Many varied life experiences will be sought but, in the end, family is everything to this lovely person, so they will always rise to action when required. When hurt, they will have a good cry, but they're able to quickly dry their eyes and get back into the swing of things. Ideally, they will have a caring job that uses words; perhaps they'll work as a teacher, counsellor, or leader of a club or group that has a supportive element. They need change and variety, but they prefer to work from the emotionally secure base of a supportive family.

GEMINI SUN/LEO MOON

This is a very outgoing, limelight-seeking person who has expensive tastes but who is great fun. They're the life and soul of the party, glib and clever with words. Leo moon adds warmth and charisma to charming Gemini, so they're a hard person to resist once they have set their heart on having you! Leo moon also gives staying power (it is a fixed sign) to relationships, but this person needs to shine at any event, so partners need to allow them to be the one on show and, while looking good on their arm, partners shouldn't steal their limelight. They're showy both in dress and with words. This combination makes for a fabulous event speaker.

GEMINI SUN/VIRGO MOON

Lighthearted yet dutiful, fun yet shy, this person will appear to be more relaxed than they are. Underneath, they worry. Like a swan on a calm lake with their legs going nineteen to the dozen under the water, their minds are always busy worrying over details. They have laser vision when it comes to finding faults, so the best careers are those that require an eye for detail. In relationships, they can be critical and nitpicky because they see everything so clearly, including their partner's faults. They're very practical and more reliable than most Geminis. They are always busy, always working, but they require little praise or support and allow partners space, so they are a good long-term prospect.

GEMINI SUN/LIBRA MOON

Quite a cool character, they're more cerebral than emotional. They like to keep life calm. Although they will have many acquaintances and friends, they keep people at an emotional distance. They prefer a light atmosphere mentally, physically, and emotionally. They have expensive tastes. Ultimately, they seek a partner who enjoys bantering and looks good on their arm. Capable and clever, they will use words in their career; they make great lawyers, but excel at any job that requires logic and a detached approach. They don't like emotional scenes and can't cope with a moody or depressive partner. They need intellectual input and airy space in relationships. They're not grounded, but they need a luxurious base to function at their best.

GEMINI SUN/SCORPIO MOON

Because they are a very deep, passionate person underneath a light and airy exterior, it is easy to be misled into thinking this person is harmless! They will be extremely capable and driven—and occasionally controlling, but only in emotional matters. They live life like a Gemini, having numerous interests, but instead of skimming the surface, they will want to dig deep and become proficient enough to converse with others and sound like they know it all. A slick outer persona hides someone completely in control, both of themselves and, ideally, of others. They are an emotionally demanding partner who expects their own freedom.

GEMINI SUN/SAGITTARIUS MOON

There is not a hope of pinning down this freedom-loving, fast-moving, hard-to-catch person. They will be fascinated by the big questions, adore travel, be quick to learn languages, talk as if there is no tomorrow, have hundreds of friends from all over the world, and never be in the same place for long. Keep a bag always packed if you attach yourself to this person, and don't expect a commitment. They need to be free to go on adventures, but they also need a partner they can talk to from dusk til dawn about the meaning of life. However, they have no interest in stability or the long-term.

GEMINI SUN/CAPRICORN MOON

Capricorn moon provides grounding for Gemini sun, so this is a hardworking, determined, ambitious person under a light outer persona. Scratch the surface of this chatty, charming, fun person and you will discover they are not light at all! They have their eye on being at the top of their profession. They're not overly warm or affectionate, yet they're reliable and security-driven in relationships. This Gemini will make a commitment and stay around. Neither sign is emotional, and they lack an adventurous spirit, but this person makes up for it with their mental energy and staying power in life.

GEMINI SUN/AQUARIUS MOON

This combination creates a real oddball in the nicest sense of the word. Quirky, funny, with a great sense of humour and a unique take on life, this person will never do what is expected or follow any rules. They will seek a similarly unusual partner who surprises (or shocks) those around them. It's best not to make any demands of this double air sign, as they must live life to their own tune, which will be out of step with everyone else's. Partners will need to be relaxed and laidback and allow them complete freedom. In that case, they stay put—but in a very loose way—because Aquarius is a fixed sign. They will use words in their career, and very cleverly.

GEMINI SUN/PISCES MOON

Both a talker and a dreamer, it will be really hard to pin down this lovely person because both signs are mutable. Therefore, this is someone who never believes tomorrow what they believe today, whose opinions and moods change from one moment to the next, and who lives life in a muddle in every way: physically, mentally, and emotionally. They are very cool emotionally, yet empathic and understanding, so they will listen sympathetically to your problems—at an emotional distance. They're not able to be of practical help; they have enough difficulty managing the practical aspects of their own lives. They need a tolerant, understanding partner who can provide grounding.

CANCER SUN/MOON COMBINATIONS

Cancer is a very emotional, caring sign, but Cancers can be over-sensitive at times. An earth moon will provide grounding, air moons give the ability to see things from a more logical perspective, and fire moons will provide a tougher inner core to help ride the ups and downs of life.

CANCER SUN/ARIES MOON

A lovely mix of energy and enthusiasm with a caring, protective nature. This person seeks to create emotional security but has an independent streak that may make them fickle, so they may lose all they have worked so hard to create if they act too impulsively. After disasters, they are able to pick themselves up and start again because they have great courage and stamina. They are a great partner because they are fun but also able to understand and sympathise. They're hardworking and family-minded, but they need to have time alone now and then. They can be tough when it's required, but they're always supportive.

CANCER SUN/TAURUS MOON

This person is very protective and caring, totally committed and focused on home and family. They are reliable, trustworthy, and compassionate. They alternate between stubborn implacability and bouts of emotionalism, which can create confusion in partners who see them as the strong, silent type. In reality, they have tender hearts. They lack a bit of adventurousness, but overall they are a solid person with traditional views. This makes them a great long-term partner.

CANCER SUN/GEMINI MOON

A perplexing mix of emotion and detachment—that's how others will perceive this person. Cancer's forte is a career where they care for others, but this sun/moon combination will be caring in a logical, cerebral way, so they would make a better scientific researcher than a hands-on carer. Better still, this could be someone who sells the latest drugs or fronts a pharmaceutical company. In short, they need to be of use to humankind in some way, but because of their Gemini moon, they also need movement and conversation. In relationships, they are protective and caring one minute, then need to step back for personal space the next. They are limited in what they can offer. Their Gemini moon makes them witty, with a great sense of humour.

CANCER SUN/CANCER MOON

Very emotional, very protective, and very compassionate. This person is liable to be easily moved by any sad story and will seek to protect the whole of mankind from the world's woes. They are deeply concerned with emotional security, and they are incredibly wounded by unkind remarks because they are very sentimental and sensitive. They can be moody, but they're very capable and self-sufficient. They are inclined to wallow and feel sorry for themselves, but they always rally in the end. Having a sun and moon in Cancer makes them incredibly devoted to loved ones. They would benefit from a more earthy partner to ground them, or a fire sign partner who can lift them out of the emotional doldrums.

CANCER SUN/LEO MOON

This is a loving person who needs a huge amount of praise for the considerable amount of work they do. Caring and protective, they do all they can for those they love, but they need to be constantly reassured that their efforts are appreciated, otherwise they can feel very aggrieved and sorry for themselves. Although they will resist leaving a committed relationship, partners will be left in no doubt if they are not happy. They adore partying and socialising, and they need to dress up and have fun now and then. Leo moon will rouse Cancer from its occasional bouts of moody emotionalism, so this person is less likely to wallow in self-pity than most Cancer suns, but partners need to praise them often to bring out their very best. Family is everything to them, but they expect to be appreciated and looked up to.

CANCER SUN/VIRGO MOON

A super balance of kindness and practicality makes for a really supportive partner and parent. This is someone who is compassionate and caring but also attends to the details. They're happy to roll up their sleeves and do what is required for anyone who needs them. As a shy but capable person, they may get a bit critical at times and worry about things, but they are genuinely nice and really care. They are a lovely partner, but they need a more adventurous mate to dig them out of work-mode and take them out to have fun. They're very selective when it comes to their friends and expect total support from them.

CANCER SUN/LIBRA MOON

This is a capable, successful person who needs to be protected from the grittier side of life. In return they will be a sympathetic, understanding, and emotional partner who is totally supportive. This person will look for a mate who is a step above, so they are quite capable of marrying for money. They will create a home that is a peaceful haven from the outside world. Often, they will find themselves providing emotional support to family and friends. This is because they are very clever at resolving arguments and keeping the peace, both at work and home. If they get the right amount of comfort and security, they can put up with almost anything and still be angelic.

CANCER SUN/SCORPIO MOON

This is a deeply emotional and easily wounded person, so it's hard to avoid stepping on their tender toes. A relationship with this person might involve walking on eggshells sometimes. They are totally driven to find emotional security, but they're also suspicious and jealous, so it's not easy for partners to convince them they are genuine and have no agenda. This is a high-drama person who is emotionally needy and demanding of reassurance. When they find someone to trust, they will be incredibly supportive and protective. They will fight to the death for those they love, but partners should be aware that life with a Cancer sun,

Scorpio moon is going to be dramatic and very emotionally demanding.

CANCER SUN/SAGITTARIUS MOON

Sagittarius will lift Cancer's occasional moodiness and inspire them to do something different, so these signs combined make for a very capable, caring person who is open to adventure and the call of the wild. They will have many friends, and they will always be there for them with understanding and sympathy. Their patience will be limited, though, so they will offer support but then expect others to get on with it. Their career would ideally lead them to a foreign place but involve a caring aspect; perhaps charitable or humanitarian medical work. They make fun partners because they are caring but have an adventurous streak.

CANCER SUN/CAPRICORN SUN

Very driven and capable, these are very family-minded people who will not only work incredibly hard for their loved ones, but will be emotionally supportive and protective too. They are a great partner and parent who tries their level best to provide everything they can for their family; they can work long hours and still get home in time to cook an evening meal. They love tradition and need both financial and emotional security, but they may sink into the doldrums without a livelier partner who takes them away from their duties now and then.

CANCER SUN/AQUARIUS MOON

This person will have a huge group of friends from all walks of life and will offer a genuinely supportive atmosphere for them. This is an interesting combination because they are emotionally needy, yet require personal space. Thus, they're more inclined to be a part of a group and keep personal partners at bay. Work-wise, they seek a career with a humanitarian aspect, and coupled with Cancer's caring side, they will aim to do something in life that makes a difference to others. Outwardly, they are capable and caring, but emotionally, they are a bit cool. They need a partner they can talk to.

CANCER SUN/PISCES MOON

A water sun and moon makes for a deeply emotional person who trusts only their instincts. Highly intuitive and probably psychic, there will be a tendency to wallow in emotions and feel overwhelmed by the needs of others. Very caring, sweet, considerate, and kind, they would benefit from a strong, earthy partner who can ground them, provide financial security, and protect them from being swamped by the demands of others. They're very easily upset by unkind remarks toward them or those they love, but they always forgive, given time.

LEO SUN/MOON COMBINATIONS

Leo shines with warmth and charisma but is needy for appreciation. Having an earth moon will provide common sense and stability, an air moon will bestow a sense of detached logic, and a water moon will instil a deeper emotional quality to their personality—but fire moons will inflate their own fire element to make a larger-than-life persona with little interest in other's sensitivities.

LEO SUN/ARIES MOON

This is one fiery, active, sporty person who loves being the centre of attention. They are determined to be number one because they are totally self-absorbed. And they're simply the most fun person to go out with. Very charismatic, warm, and charming on the surface, but they can be proud, stubborn, determined, and opinionated. They have to have their own way, which makes them inclined to be bossy. They are also very protective of loved ones and will face any danger on their behalf without a second thought. They have an incredibly buoyant personality, as they are able to face any obstacle and overcome it. This person will need a more grounded partner, as they are not at all practical.

LEO SUN/TAURUS MOON

This combination of fire and earth makes for a great partner who is warm and loving, sensuous, and very protective. But both signs are fixed, so they are also an incredibly stubborn person. Overall, they're realistic and security-minded. They like cuddles and being in a partnership; closeness is important. Both signs like a bit of luxury, so they will adore going away to grand hotels and living the high life for a while. This combination will work hard to improve their financial situation so they can continue to enjoy the best things in life. A sexy, adaptable partner would suit them, but they must be able to look the part when going out and about. This person needs constant praise.

LEO SUN/GEMINI MOON

This person loves to be where it's at. They're a seeker of the high life, and they also have the desire to mix with people who are making the world what it is today. Preferably, though, they will *be* one of those people. With their artistic ability, their desire to shine and stand out, their clever way with words, and their up-to-date knowledge, they will be very much in demand. They need a classy, glamorous partner who looks good and who adores them, but who won't be too clingy. Security and tradition are meaningless to them; it is the now that appeals. They're likely to have more than one long-term relationship, as they enjoy having someone gorgeous beside them.

LEO SUN/CANCER MOON

Their attention will be focused on their house and family, both of which will need to be better than anyone else's. Very loving, very protective, and extremely caring under a charismatic exterior, they will want their partner and children to be always well-dressed, well-behaved, and a step up from the norm. They're quite sensitive but too proud to show it. They need an earthy partner to ground them and create some much-needed financial security, as they like to spend money both on their home and themselves. They will need constant reassurance of their partner's love.

LEO SUN/LEO MOON

Wow, this is one fiery, charming, and charismatic person! Full of warmth and love, they seek the very best life has to offer. They will do anything to be in the limelight and strive to be acknowledged as great at what they do. They cannot live an ordinary life—it must be a grand sweep, a dramatic life full of admiration. Because they are very self-sufficient and self-centred, a partner is only there to make them look good (and to continually stroke their ego). Yet, they do make loving partners, and because they are a fixed sign, they may stick around if they get the right amount of praise and admiration. An actor through and through, no matter what they actually do.

LEO SUN/VIRGO MOON

Leo's need for high drama is tempered by Virgo's more shy, modest demeanour, so this is a good combination of warmth and earthiness. This person makes a genuinely lovely partner who will enjoy going out and dressing up, but will also roll up their sleeves and do the everyday tasks we all have to attend to. They're full of energy, but a bit frantic at times, so it might be hard to stop them from overdoing things. They will be body-conscious, so diets and exercise will be important to them, as they want to look their best. They may worry about details, but generally, the overall picture is drawn on a large scale; they think big.

LEO SUN/LIBRA MOON

This is an extravagant mix of two luxury-loving signs, which will create someone who must have the best in life. If they can't afford the best hotels or restaurants, they won't go. If they can't afford the best house, they will make the one they have beautiful. Details are anathema to them. They can marry for money, but they are capable of working for it, as Libra moon gives them a clever mind, capable of working out ways to achieve their aims. Partners will have to be classy or they won't look twice. Neither sign is sympathetic or compassionate, though will always lend a hand if it makes them look good. They're not at all interested in the mundane aspects of life and expect someone else to do all that.

LEO SUN/SCORPIO MOON

A combination of two strong signs creates a deeply passionate, driven, and ambitious person who seeks a partner who gives their all—just as they do. They require a dramatic life in every sense, so everything will be made larger than it is to drag every ounce of passion, emotion, and love from the moment. They are a hard partner to satisfy because they need complete loyalty and plenty of lust as well as someone who looks sultry and attractive. They're totally in control and often bossy, so they need someone flexible and easygoing, as they are always number one, both at home and work.

LEO SUN/SAGITTARIUS MOON

Two fire signs make this a fast, impulsive combination. This is a wild, freedom-seeking, restless person who is incredibly sociable and will have hundreds of friends. They're almost impossible to pin down to a place or time, yet they need to love and be loved, so they might stop long enough to grab a partner—as long as they're allowed personal freedom and offered an adoring amount of praise. It would be helpful if potential partners had money or, at the very least, were grounded, as someone needs to stay home and attend to the chores!

LEO SUN/CAPRICORN MOON

Both of these signs want the best in life, but Capricorn moon is more than willing to put in the hours to achieve their aim. More traditional and grounded than most Leos, this perfect pairing of energy, drive, and ambition means they could go far; they expect a number one slot with copious admiration from their peers. Partners will need to look the part, but as Capricorn is aiming high in life, a classy look would be best. This person has stamina and staying power, but they might need to be reminded that there is more to life than the big picture. They're not emotional or empathic, but when they commit, it will be forever.

LEO SUN/AQUARIUS MOON

This person prefers to be a little aloof when it comes to emotional matters, so they're better in large groups than one-on-one. Leo needs love, and both signs are fixed, so they will certainly make commitments, but they might wander off when their partner needs some practical help. It would help, then, if a partner was grounded and stable and allowed this lovely, zany, sparkling diamond their space, then welcomed them home with a hug. It is unlikely this person will stray, despite their love of the limelight, but partners should expect to deal with the minutiae of life, as this person won't even see what needs to be done.

LEO SUN/PISCES MOON

An artistic dreamer, this is a ready-made musician, artist, sculptor, or similar who goes by their gut-feeling and intuition. They are quite shy, yet they're capable of rising to the occasion when required. They would love to be recognised for their artistic endeavours, but they are so kind, helpful, warm, and loving that they will always make the best of whatever life throws at them. They have a way of getting others to do things for them, as they appear quite fragile or incapable. A supportive, financially astute partner would be useful, although success in the world is possible as long as they follow their inner artistic voice.

VIRGO SUN/MOON COMBINATIONS

Virgo is a kind, dutiful, hardworking earth sign who often gets sidetracked by details. A fire moon is a great combination because it provides some physical courage and daring. An air moon will make them more critical but slightly detached. An earth moon will make them a bit too staid. A water moon will make them the best they can be; they're not only kind, but genuinely empathic and caring.

VIRGO SUN/ARIES MOON

A very direct and outspoken combination. Virgo sees all mistakes and Aries will find it hard not to say it how it is, so they will need an easygoing, tolerant partner. However, they are actually very kind, honest, and driven. They are so hardworking they could be considered workaholics, so a partner will need to drag them away on a holiday now and then to get them away from things they feel they must do. They're quite critical, but they don't really mean to be unkind; they just see hundreds of things to do and get frustrated with being slowed down by life's minutiae. They're emotionally insensitive, but not because they don't care; they just can't abide drama.

VIRGO SUN/TAURUS MOON

Both are earth signs, so this is a very hardworking person who gives their all to create financial security for themselves and loved ones. They're very grounded, security driven, and stubborn, but they will make a good parent. They enjoy nature in all its forms. This person is deeply sensuous and touchy-feely; they love cuddles and are a highly-sexed partner. They may lack imagination and an adventurous spirit, but they make up for it with oodles of love and plenty of stability. Inclined to nitpick and worry, they would never ever leave a committed relationship, They are adept at the repetitive tasks of a household, so they usually end up with an air or fire sign partner who can lighten their mood.

VIRGO SUN/GEMINI MOON

Both Virgo and Gemini are ruled by Mercury, so there is emphasis on communication. Both signs are also mutable, so it will be hard to pin down this person. Virgo sun is hardworking, so they will make sure the jobs are done, but they can get overly fussy, nitpicky, and critical when they feel trapped or overworked. Virgo is hard to please when looking for a partner and Gemini hates commitment, so relationships may be a difficult area. Ultimately, they need a partner who can keep up with their ideas and need for variety, but who can provide interesting verbal input—and someone with a thick skin, because their tongue will be brutally waspish at times. Partners will have to drag them away from work so they can relax.

VIRGO SUN/CANCER MOON

For this combination, family is the be-all and end-all. Very loving and caring, supportive, and hardworking, though they are sensitive and easily hurt under their logical exterior. They make a great partner and parent because they are kind, modest, and very capable. They attend to all the chores and duties of home and family, and they are also compassionate and supportive of loved ones. However, they will get moody and critical when tired. When that happens, partners need to take them on holiday to get them away from their responsibilities.

VIRGO SUN/LEO MOON

This is an apparently modest person, but they secretly enjoy attention and the limelight. They work incredibly hard and don't mind doing the dull jobs, but they prefer delegating. Even so, they will notice everything and point out missed bits! Whatever they do, they will expect to be thanked. Nevertheless, they are loyal, warm, dutiful, and kind. This combination creates the least modest of the Virgo suns because Leo loves to party and be noticed, so this is someone who will be glamorous and fun when the work is done. They're sexy, too, with great charisma.

VIRGO SUN/VIRGO MOON

This double Virgo makes for someone who finds it hard to stop worrying and let go of chores. They're particular and fussy, and they're inclined to be sharply critical, so they will need a partner who can lighten the atmosphere and surprise them with special trips away. Virgo won't want to leave until their jobs are done, though, so their partner might need to pack their bag and literally pull them out the door! They are very dutiful and attentive partners. They're extremely modest during the day, but earthy and sexy in private. They tend to get bogged down by details, so a calm, logical mate with a sense of humour will help them relax.

VIRGO SUN/LIBRA MOON

A classy, cool person who sees every fault. Fussy, elegant, and comfort-loving, they would prefer not to mix with those who are imperfect, so they have high and exacting standards when seeking a partner. They desire someone who can protect them from the harsh realities of life. Even so, they will do their best to make sure jobs are done, but they dream of a world where they have staff! Very clever and logical, but they like a peaceful, calm, undisturbed existence. Partners need to be as beautiful and organised as they are. Preferably, they will find a fire sign to take them on adventures; otherwise, they can adopt a lazy lifestyle.

VIRGO SUN/SCORPIO MOON

This is one sexy combination! Earthy, sensuous Virgo and passionate Scorpio creates someone for whom the bedroom assumes great significance. They are driven by jealous passions but hide it under a calm, logical, apparently dutiful exterior. Partners can be misled into thinking they are less passionate and driven than they are. Don't be fooled—this person is a spider in a web just waiting for an unsuspecting fly! They make good long-term partners as long as they are able to indulge their physical side, but they are emotionally controlling and very cautious when it comes to bestowing their hearts.

VIRGO SUN/SAGITTARIUS MOON

Both signs are mutable, so commitment will be a challenge for them. Virgo will always be working and Sagittarius needs personal freedom, so this creates a fun, fiery, friendly person with an earthy passion who doesn't want to be tied down—or someone who might commit in a weak moment, but then feels the sudden need to walk away. This combination creates quite a complicated character who is edgy, fidgety, outspoken, and restless. A tolerant partner is required!

VIRGO SUN/AQUARIUS MOON

A very cool, detached, friendly person who enjoys meeting up with others, but who is hard to please in relationships. They prefer a bit of distance and, while apparently modest and dutiful, don't connect very deeply to anyone. They are able to live and let live, yet they're also hard-working, so jobs get done. They will become snappy and irritable when tired or overworked. They need personal freedom and like to shock now and then, so they will do something outrageous just for the hell of it, which sits strangely on one who is normally quite shy. Partners will struggle to understand them, but it's likely they won't even understand themselves!

VIRGO SUN/PISCES MOON

This is a very kind, sensitive, and caring person who really does their best for others in every way they can. This combination is capable of more hard work than most Pisceans (and certainly tidier), but they are a complicated mix of logic and intuition. There is a limit to their compassion and energy, as they tend to drift off into a dream world and lose track of themselves. This is the sort of person who writes lists, then loses them; who starts jobs, then wanders off before they are completed. Quite shy, they need a partner who can look after them and on whom they can lean. At times, they have a snappy, critical tongue, especially when they are tired.

LIBRA SUN/MOON COMBINATIONS

Libra is a luxury-loving, logical, harmony-seeking sign who would benefit from greater emotional depth, so a Libra sun works well when combined with a water moon, as it produces someone both logical and empathic. Air moons heighten their intellectual capacity. Fire moons can make them a bit insensitive. Earth moons work well, as they are grounding, but this air/earth mix also intensifies their need for the material benefits of life.

LIBRA SUN/ARIES MOON

These two opposing signs create an outer demeanour that is cool and calm, but underneath they are driven and argumentative. They may appear compromising, but they are determined to have their own way, and they are not always able to back down. Both signs are cardinal, so this person has lots of drive and energy and is able to perform well in life. They're emotionally warm once you scratch the surface, but neither sign is compassionate, and Aries can be insensitive. This is quite a selfish combination because Libra, although geared toward compromise, will only do so if they get the material rewards they seek. So, in this pairing, their own comfort and desire takes top place.

LIBRA SUN/TAURUS MOON

Both signs need comfort and security, so this person's drive will be to make money so they can enjoy all the luxuries of life. A large house and a big bank balance are required to ensure peace of mind. Both signs are ruled by Venus, so their house will be beautifully furnished with the focus on both comfort and style. Taurus loves food, so they will indulge, but Libra will prefer they do so at a classy restaurant! Sensuous but sometimes cool, and with a tendency to be lazy, they seek a rich partner for keeps.

LIBRA SUN/GEMINI MOON

Two detached air signs make for a fun, entertaining, intelligent socialite who needs intellectual stimulation in a partner, but who must also look good. They will seek a really high-end lifestyle where they can be at the forefront of what's going on. They love anything to do with celebrity and fashion and will dress to impress, so they're always classy and stylish. They're not interested in longevity in a relationship and will avoid arguments and scenes. One day, they may simply disappear during conflict—though this combination will stay with their partner if they help provide the lifestyle they enjoy.

LIBRA SUN/CANCER MOON

A lovely homemaker with compassion and a caring manner. They love family and children. Libra desires to keep life peaceful and calm, so they will endeavour to create beautiful surroundings and extend energy toward being compromising; they will teach children to do the same. They're looking for the perfect family and the perfect home. Both signs are hardworking and driven, so they can manage their career and their home life, but they need a partner for emotional security. Nevertheless, they will only chose someone who looks good *and* who will provide supportive love for the family.

LIBRA SUN/LEO MOON

Nothing but the high life for this combination! They love luxury and want to stand out from the crowd, so they enjoy wearing designer fashion. They want to live life on a grand and luxurious scale, especially because they would adore being feted and praised. They're one of life's beautiful people. Similarly, they will seek an attractive partner who looks good on their arm. They're not really interested in family life, although if they do settle down, they will expect their children to be on display as well, and will use them as accessories.

LIBRA SUN/VIRGO MOON

This is a calm, sensible person who is no fool. They will be hard to catch romantically, as Libra is discerning and Virgo cautious. They won't give their heart to just anyone. Both signs can work hard, though they have exacting standards in every aspect of life and can be quite judgmental and critical. Because they lack an adventurous spirit, a fire sign mate could bring some fun into their lives and pull them away from their narrow mindset, but they will be hard to please. They seek a better-than-average lifestyle and select only intellectual/financial equals as friends.

LIBRA SUN/LIBRA MOON

This person is full of Venusian charm, but they're also cool and crisp—almost icy at times. They are absolutely determined to live in the best way possible, and they're able to create it through their own efforts because they are extremely balanced, logical, and intellectual. This combination makes for a great lawyer or mediator. Airy and sensible, they're not swayed by emotions or passion—quite the opposite: they prefer no drama. They are very sociable and seek a classy partner, though they're not interested in a traditional partnership because they have no intention of getting their hands dirty with menial tasks. They would prefer a millionaire lifestyle.

LIBRA SUN/SCORPIO MOON

A complex mix: cool detachment rests on the surface, but passions boil underneath. They are liable to draw people in with their charm and then reveal a jealous, suspicious nature not akin to first impressions. They need a deep emotional attachment with a mate who brings both passion and the ability to provide for the luxuries Libra requires. They won't settle for just anyone; they seek someone who worships them and puts them on a pedestal, who will both adore them and keep them removed from the grittier side of life. They might be too self-absorbed to want a family, as Scorpio moons are focused solely on their own needs.

LIBRA SUN/SAGITTARIUS MOON

This is someone who is elegant and calm, cool, and reserved on the surface, but wilder than they appear. Sagittarius needs freedom and speaks their mind, so although Libra can spend a long time building the lovely life they require, a Sagittarius moon might feel the need to be free and start from scratch on a whim. They are constantly vying between the need for a partner and the need for freedom, which makes this an unreliable but exciting mix in a partnership. They're very sociable and have hundreds of friends, but be wary of asking their opinion, because they will be extraordinarily blunt. A relaxed, tolerant air sign would suit them well.

LIBRA SUN/CAPRICORN MOON

This is a very driven mix. This person is determined to rise high and reach the top of their profession. They have an eye for class in all aspects and won't settle for anything/anyone less than the very best. They require a partner who won't shame them when they reach the dizzying heights of their ambitions. Appearance is everything, but even so, they are clever, intellectual, and hardworking, so they will achieve all they desire through sheer persistence. They're emotionally reserved and cool, but they do need a reason for all their efforts, so they want a family.

LIBRA SUN/AQUARIUS MOON

When it comes to relationships, this combination is more about friendship. Both Libra and Aquarius are air signs, so this person is sociable, with a classy surface hiding a quirky sense of humour and a desire to shock. Their friends will come from all walks of life: Libra is usually very selective of who they mix with, but an Aquarius moon means anything is possible, as they love doing the unexpected! It's very hard to emotionally tie them down, but Libra does need a partner, so they will choose someone classy who is different in some way. They need a very tolerant, hardworking, and good-looking partner who can attend to the details of life. With that being said, this combination is apt to walk out when life gets stressful, as both signs abhor drama and emotionalism.

LIBRA SUN/PISCES MOON

This is a very attractive, kind person who is compassionate but cool. They can offer advice but have limited physical stamina. Their energy levels are prone to extremes; they may veer from being busy to not being able to get out of bed. Ideally, they would like a luxurious life with no stresses, so they tend to look to others to do the chores. This complex interweaving of a logical sun and an intuitive, dreamy moon means they are often their own worst enemy because common sense often deserts them just when they need it most, yet sometimes they do come up with a surprisingly good solution to a problem. A supportive partner who looks after them is sought. Although they have good intentions, this is not someone who can be leaned on or relied upon.

SCORPIO SUN/MOON COMBINATIONS

Because Scorpio sun is so enigmatic and secretive, it's unlikely the moon sign, whatever it may be, will be exposed to others at all! Fire moons are unstoppable combined with Scorpio and provide them with drive, physical energy, and the ability to get back on track after setbacks. Air moons are helpful because they provide some cool logic, and earth moons provide common sense and are grounding. But another water moon will be a hard combination for others to live with: it heightens the already-dramatic quality of Scorpio's emotions.

SCORPIO SUN/ARIES MOON

Motives will be disguised, but this person loves the chase. Challenge is everything, both in their career and relationships. They're determined to get to the top, but they must be self-employed or work alone, as they are not team players. They're passionate and affectionate but are determined to keep their emotional independence, so they're a hard person to break through to romantically. They keep others at bay and find it hard to care about them. They're a bit insensitive and careless of other's hearts, but nevertheless, they seek complete control of relationships while remaining autonomous. Others may perceive them as pompous.

SCORPIO SUN/TAURUS MOON

Both of these signs are sensuous, so this combination creates a very sexy, passionate person for whom partnership is paramount. They love both the physical and emotional expressions of love, so they are incredibly romantic—but they expect their romance to end up in bed. They seek emotional and financial security, and what they own will be of the greatest importance. They're destined to have considerable wealth. Partners might find living with this combination is like being under house arrest, as both signs are possessive and controlling in different ways. There may not be much room for partners to manoeuvre, but they will be provided for in heaps.

SCORPIO SUN/GEMINI MOON

Scorpio will enjoy controlling every situation, both at work and at home, and Gemini will give them a caustic way with words when annoyed or upset, so this is someone who can use their tongue as a weapon. This mix of the superficial and the deep means they will pursue many hobbies and interests, and they will explore them in depth. Generally, this person is a lighter Scorpio who will enjoy the social side of life and playing with words in a clever, sometimes amusing way—though partners may sometimes be the butt of the joke. Laugh even if it kills you!

SCORPIO SUN/CANCER MOON

A deeply emotional and sensitive pairing of two water signs make this someone very easily hurt by the words or actions of others. Ultra-fragile emotionally, it might be like walking on eggshells, and Scorpio will want to retaliate when hurt. They need emotional security and to focus love on one person. They will be incredibly loyal and protective of family and very compassionate and understanding, but they will be hard to truly know, and they are a very emotionally demanding partner to please because they require constant reassurance that they are loved. With this combination, life is all about them and their needs, but the partner who provides this attention will be adored with a passion.

SCORPIO SUN/LEO MOON

Here is someone who needs to be recognised on the stage of life. This person is very in control, fixated on standing out from the crowd, and absolutely determined to shine in the limelight. Both signs are fixed, so they're also incredibly stubborn and will never back down. They are passionate and warm to partners, but they are always number one and expect to be shown respect and admiration. They also expect partners to give them heaps of praise, even though they already know they are the best. They can be arrogant, but partners should do their best to tolerate their bossiness, as this person will lead an exciting life indeed.

SCORPIO SUN/VIRGO MOON

This person will be extraordinarily laser-eyed. Nothing is missed—every detail is noted. Dutiful, hardworking, and driven, underneath a calm exterior lurks one of the most passionate people you are ever likely to meet. They're a bit more logical than most Scorpios, but they're also extremely critical and have high expectations of everyone, especially partners. This is a particularly hard nut to crack when it comes to love, especially because they are so selective of all the people they allow into their lives. They're extremely sexy at the right time, which is once every task has been completed.

SCORPIO SUN/LIBRA MOON

This person is determined to live life in luxury. Both signs like the best, but both can work hard for it; neither will want anything to do with the underbelly of life. They will be incredibly choosy when it comes to their partners, and they expect someone who looks and sounds good. They're very sociable, yet they're a hard person to know, as Scorpio keeps secrets. Libra moon will calm some of the sun's more extravagant passions, so they are emotionally cooler than most Scorpios, but a relationship will still be challenging because of their mixture of detachment and passion. Very clever and astute, they seek logical, balanced answers to all questions. They prefer keeping the peace and endeavour to please all people all the time, so they often placate partners; this is unusual for a Scorpio sun, as they normally enjoy a bit of drama.

SCORPIO SUN/SCORPIO MOON

This is one passionate, intense, deep, and emotionally driven person who will live life to the max. Partners will find it hard to keep up with their sex drive and emotional games. They're very self-protective, so it's extremely hard to break through to the real person underneath; it may take years to really know them, if at all. They're prone to jealous suspicions, mind games, and subtle manipulation. They will succeed in life because of their sheer determination, but partners will have to be tough to survive. For Scorpio moons, it's all about their emotional needs being met, so partners need to always be available and not busy doing other things when this moon sign starts wallowing.

SCORPIO SUN/SAGITTARIUS MOON

A combination of fire and water makes this person a complex mix of a deeply passionate nature with a desire for personal freedom. They might have a family but are determined to be a free spirit emotionally, though they do need a partner on whom to focus their considerable sex drive. It is best that they choose a partner who will tolerate their wanderings as they search for the meaning of life; Scorpio and Sagittarius together make a powerhouse of research and investigation. Beware crossing this person: Scorpio always takes revenge, and Sagittarius is brutal with words, and neither are sensitive of the feelings of others.

SCORPIO SUN/CAPRICORN MOON

A heavy mix of emotional passion and steely ambition makes this person a workaholic who is determined to reach the highest pinnacle of success in their career. They are very serious and very driven, with a single-minded focus. They're also rather secretive about their aims, which leaves little time for fun and frolics. They need a lighter, more fun partner to drag them away from their desk and show them there is another world out there, far away from work. They do not undertake anything lightly, prefer to work alone, and are destined to succeed at whatever they aim for.

SCORPIO SUN/AQUARIUS MOON

This is a complicated person who needs both emotional intensity and personal space. They could veer between one or the other, which will be confusing for partners. Work-wise, they are capable of breakthroughs in research projects, as Aquarius thinks obliquely and Scorpio delves to the depths. This is someone unique and special, and they need a tolerant partner who can attend to the more prosaic aspects of life so they are free to excel in whatever field they chose. They're not a hands-on family person, but they do want a stable relationship. They're also very stubborn and determined to be themselves, so partners take second place.

SCORPIO SUN/PISCES MOON

This is a very sensitive and sexy person who will be incredibly self-protective because of their extreme vulnerabilities. They are more empathic and compassionate to others than Scorpios usually are. They need a calm, grounded partner who will provide oodles of affection and plenty of stability because sometimes they lose their way emotionally, plagued as they are by all sorts of suspicions and intuitive interplays. They often assume more is going on than is the case, so they can get paranoid. Because they are a very emotional person, they need to be alone to allow their passions to calm now and then. They're probably psychic, but they keep any visions to themselves.

SAGITTARIUS SUN/MOON COMBINATIONS

Sagittarius is a freedom-loving fire sign who hates being fettered in any way. Earth moons will steady them, air moons provide much-needed logic and detachment, water moons help them connect with others emotionally, and fire moons will create a real wild child who must be free.

SAGITTARIUS SUN/ARIES MOON

Two brash fire signs make this a wild one, forever rushing in where angels fear to tread. Incredibly impulsive, impatient, restless, freedom-seeking, and lacking in empathy, they will live life to their own tune and don't really need others. They come across as a warm, very friendly person with loads of friends, but it is impossible to tie them down to a long-term commitment. It's best if they work for themselves, as they cannot abide rules and restrictions. They're brutally honest but well-intentioned, and affectionate too! But personal freedom is paramount.

SAGITTARIUS SUN/TAURUS MOON

Despite appearing restless and impatient on the surface, they need a stable love life and a sturdy bank balance to feel secure. They will create a safe base and then head out to explore. This is a reliable Sagittarian with a sense of adventure and fun; they love travel, but they also need affection and cuddles and to know someone will be at home waiting for them when they return. They will endeavour to make money from their adventures. Once they've settled on a partner, they won't leave them, but they will try their partner's patience with their need for both stability and freedom!

SAGITTARIUS SUN/GEMINI MOON

These two mutable signs, when linked, create someone who must be free and unfettered. They're very adaptable, restless, changeable, and unreliable, but they're also clever, fun, and adventurous. They are unlikely to settle for long because they need to move around, mentally and physically. A seeker of the meaning of life and a messenger of the first order, words and learning are their be-all and end-all. Intellectual with occasional bouts of warmth, they will attract a huge number of friends, but stable relationships will try their patience.

SAGITTARIUS SUN/CANCER MOON

This is someone pulled between creating emotional security and yet wanting to be free to roam the world. They might be able to manage both, if they find the right partner who can cope with their restless yet emotional stance on life. Everything they learn will feel deeply personal, and they will love history, so they would make good historians, archaeologists, and lost-family researchers. They will enjoy travel, but they'll call home regularly to check if all is well. At the end of the day, they need a family to come home to, and they need to know what they do in life makes a difference.

SAGITTARIUS SUN/LEO MOON

This double fire sign seeks the limelight. Leo seeks a stage and Sagittarius is happy being in the public eye, so it's likely they will end up as a foreign correspondent or travel journalist or similar; they must travel and be free to roam, but they want to be recognised and applauded for their work. A love of languages, foreign cultures, and esoteric subjects makes it likely something in this vein will be their focus. They can manage a commitment but will need plenty of freedom and a lot of praise/admiration to keep them happy.

SAGITTARIUS SUN/VIRGO MOON

This is a more practical, dutiful Sagittarius who has a great eye for detail. They're able to spot things others have missed, so they are great at researching old documents. On the outside they are a friendly, sociable person, but they're actually a little shy when it comes to personal matters. They need a reliable partner at home when they head off on their travels. They're very adaptable so they can fit in anywhere, and they will be less blunt than most Sagittarians because of their innate consideration.

SAGITTARIUS SUN/LIBRA MOON

Very sociable and fun, this person adores being with friends and chatting. Ideally, they will have a big, beautifully furnished house that they can show off. They have a larger-than-life appetite for the best things and an innate sense they will be looked after by the universe. Restless but very clever, they will need a partner but will never feel totally committed, veering between warmth and coolness, which can be confusing for loved ones. They're liable to continually overspend, but it will be hard for partners to get annoyed because of their charm.

SAGITTARIUS SUN/SCORPIO MOON

This is a moody, changeable person who is pulled between their deep desires and the need to feel personally free. Scorpio moon needs a complete blending with another, while Sagittarius is restless and impulsive. On the surface, then, they are a relaxed, busy person with loads of friends, but underneath deep passions lurk. Generally, they will keep things secretive, but don't ask for their opinion because when they give it, it will be brutal. They will be inclined to want control of others while maintaining their own personal freedoms.

SAGITTARIUS SUN/SAGITTARIUS MOON

This is a wild child, with a restless, impulsive, fiery nature who must be completely free of ties. A risk-taker with an innate belief they will always find their feet and have what they need, they are self-sufficient and driven, though they do scatter their energies all over the place. They're always on the move. They have hundreds of friends, sociable and unfettered as they are, and it's hard not to like them, but beware of bestowing your heart, as they cannot commit. They're also brutally honest, so don't ask for their opinion unless you can take it on the chin!

SAGITTARIUS SUN/CAPRICORN MOON

Capricorn moon will make sure Sagittarius's travels and adventures are turned into a profitable business. They seek to make money from their research and teaching; their ideal occupation is one that pays them to explore. Under a more free-thinking outer persona, they are driven and ambitious. They're very grounded and sensible, and they will definitely settle down because they need tradition and security to give them a reason for all their hard work. They are destined to succeed in some form of research. They adore ancient subjects with a long history and make great teachers at higher-education levels.

SAGITTARIUS SUN/AQUARIUS MOON

This is a real wild child in every sense. Freedom-loving and slightly wacky with a desire to shock, heaven knows what they will say next! Sagittarians are blunt anyway, but adding unpredictable Aquarius into the mix makes for a very unusual oddball in the nicest sense of the word. They don't need others much, although they do prefer friendship to partnership. This is because they need to keep things light and fun; emotional drama is not their thing at all. But it's hard not to like them, as they're very sociable, easygoing, and nonjudgmental. However, they're totally unreliable and unpredictable in relationships. An earthy partner might ground them just a little, or at least make sure there is a home to come back to when they finally return from their wanderings.

SAGITTARIUS SUN/PISCES MOON

This is a more sensitive Sagittarius who is understanding and compassionate, but neither sign is overly keen on commitment. Being mutable in both sun and moon, they need personal freedom, and while they can talk for hours, they can get easily overfaced by practical demands. They're a super friend, but when it comes to relationships, they need a partner who will support them in every way, and who allows them to express their strange ideas. They could be incredibly psychic; certainly, they will be drawn to esoteric subjects and feel a link to things beyond. They are convinced they are looked after by the universe and possibly believe in previous lives.

CAPRICORN SUN/MOON COMBINATIONS

Capricorn is a steady, reliable, hardworking earth sign, so it benefits from all moon signs except earth, because then the material side of life is their whole focus. An air moon provides lightness and logic, a fire moon allows them to take a few risks, and a water moon provides a greater depth of feeling for others.

CAPRICORN SUN/ARIES MOON

This is an incredibly ambitious combination, but they may prefer to work for themselves, which is unusual for a Capricorn. Driven, but with an impulsive streak, they are hardworking, hardheaded, and determined to succeed. They are not overly sympathetic or emotional, which can be tough for partners (who will have to attend to the mundane aspects of life), as Capricorn works long hours and rarely enjoys holidays. Full of energy and drive, they have incredible stamina but direct it all into material success. Emotionally, they are impatient and a bit self-centred.

CAPRICORN SUN/TAURUS MOON

This is a very worthy person, but one for whom the material aspects of life are everything. They are driven to build, build, build, and they surround themselves with luxury. They're unlikely to exit life with less than a considerable fortune, but relationships may suffer from a lack of sensitivity and attention. They are too busy working to make a great partner, but they can be sensual and do enjoy a cuddle—once they can drag themselves away from work. They are very down-to-earth and possessive of what they consider theirs, which applies to people as well as goods. Nevertheless, they will provide well for their family and do their very best.

CAPRICORN SUN/GEMINI MOON

Gemini moon makes this Capricorn far more sociable and less traditional. They still have an eye on making gains, but they're more open to modern ways and ideas, and they are able to use networking as a tool to advance their status. Nevertheless, they're a cool character, able to stand back and be sensible and logical. Because they will always be either working or chatting with others who can advance their cause, they are not the easiest partner. They have little time for personal friends and emotional matters and might be hard to pin down for long.

CAPRICORN SUN/CANCER MOON

This Capricorn is even more traditional and family-minded than usual, because Capricorn needs financial security and Cancer needs emotional security. Family will be everything, with all efforts going toward providing security for them in all aspects. Hardworking and ambitious but also protective and caring, this is a fabulous parent who does their very best for their offspring and gives them every opportunity in life. This person will expect great things from their children, though. They are a supportive and caring partner, too, so they're a good match for someone who is likewise interested in family and longevity in relationships. Underneath their capable demeanour, they will be quite insecure.

CAPRICORN SUN/LEO MOON

Here is someone who not only wants the very best in life, but to be feted for it too. An ambitious, hardworking person who adores the limelight but who is oddly, quite shy. Capricorn is a modest sign but they do love the very best life has to offer, as long as it is classy. Add to this a Leo moon who seeks constant affirmation that they are great and you have a rather needy person. Partners will have to constantly reassure them they are great, which can be tiring, but in return they will provide all the luxuries of life, and some! It is all about them, though, so partners take second place.

CAPRICORN SUN/VIRGO MOON

This double earth sign signifies a hardworking, dutiful, shy person who worries a lot. They tend to overwork themselves and then find fault with others. They are not unkind, they just find it hard to unwind, relax, and have fun. A lively partner is needed to drag them away from chores and responsibilities now and then, and to make them laugh; otherwise they get very bogged down in details and may suffer from depression. Ambitious, organised, and very business-savvy, they instinctively know the devil is in the details, so they make amazing lawyers and accountants. While they desperately want and need a reliable partner, they are not adept at social conversation, so it's more a case of someone taking pity on them!

CAPRICORN SUN/LIBRA MOON

This is a very conventional mix that brings an adept social manner to the normally shy Capricorn. This person wants the very best life has to offer in material terms. Where they live and how they live is of paramount importance; they want a large house that is beautifully furnished, and their family will always have the very best, although a lot of time will be given to appearances. However, as both signs are proactive and hardworking they are destined to succeed in their career. Libra moon needs a partner while Capricorn sun needs a family, but neither sign will settle for just anyone. For them, good manners, good looks, and a healthy bank balance are important in partners.

CAPRICORN SUN/SCORPIO MOON

Incredibly ambitious but highly secretive, no one will ever really know what this person's plan is, but they will have one—and it will be one that brings wealth and prestige. They are more passionate than most Capricorns. Under a conservative exterior lies a deep, compelling, sexy, emotionally driven person. Nothing but the best in life will do, and with their canny intellect, powerful drive, and ability to work nonstop, nothing is impossible for them to achieve. They can be possessive and controlling of partners, but their loved ones will want for nothing; this combination is someone who will both succeed materially and love with the deepest passion.

CAPRICORN SUN/SAGITTARIUS MOON

The fire of Sagittarius brings an emotional warmth to realistic, grounded Capricorn, but these two signs are so different this person is in danger of working hard and then suddenly throwing it all over, especially when the call of the wild sweeps over them. As a complex mix of traditional, dutiful Capricorn and freedom-loving, truth-seeking Sagittarius, this person will hover between their need to be emotionally free and yet financially secure. If they can harness their love of travel and foreign cultures by making it a moneymaking project, they will find greater inner happiness. Because they love exploring, they will need a partner who stays home.

CAPRICORN SUN/CAPRICORN MOON

This is someone who is incredibly ambitious, but they are so hardworking and driven that it is all work and no play, so they can come across as dull and unadventurous. They are a workaholic who doesn't know how to let their hair down, nor do they see the point. Their life is all about striving to be the best. They will settle down because everything they do is for their family, but partners will need to accept that they work long hours and that, for them, duty always comes first. They will provide considerable financial security and status, but they are lacking in social skills and have little need for fun, so it will take some skill to manoeuvre them into a holiday but partners should do their best to encourage some down time.

CAPRICORN SUN/AQUARIUS MOON

When it comes to being around groups of people, this Capricorn is better than most; they enjoy their friendships and need them in order to relax. They are still very traditional on the surface but have an odd, off-the-wall sense of humour that sometimes sits strangely, as does their need to say or do something totally out of character. They find it hard to relate at a personal level, except as a friend. Yet, Capricorn needs a family, so when they settle down, they will keep plenty of space for themselves and head off to work whenever their home life gets too demanding. Partners will have to be tolerant and understanding as this mix of stability, conservatism and eccentricity will make them a difficult person to understand.

CAPRICORN SUN/PISCES MOON

A mix of the traditional and otherworldly makes this a very sweet person who is kind and gentle under a hardworking, ambitious exterior. They will have more limited stamina than most Capricorns, who can be workaholics. Everything is for others with this combination, and Pisces moon will make them incredibly supportive and compassionate, but neither sign is warm, so they will listen, extend advice, and then retreat. This person is apt to swim off to calmer waters now and then to have time to themselves, to recover from other's demands, and, especially, the demands they place on themselves. They might benefit from a fire sign partner to bring some excitement and action into their lives.

AQUARIUS SUN/MOON COMBINATIONS

This zany, freedom-loving sign would benefit from an earth moon to bring them down to reality! Air moons will make them a totally free spirit, and fire moons provide energy and drive. But water moons are best, because they instil empathy and compassion for others.

AQUARIUS SUN/ARIES MOON

This combination will have a bit more drive and energy than most Aquarians, as well as some inner warmth, but they insist on total freedom and independence. Aries moons are quite hard and unfeeling, though they do like a hug now and then. This person is inclined to romantically leap in without thinking, but neither sign is empathic or sympathetic, so partners will need to be tough; they are not practical or family-minded. A grounded mate might survive, if they are prepared to deal with the demands of ordinary life. They have a lot of wildly impractical schemes, but one may work, if they are lucky.

AQUARIUS SUN/TAURUS MOON

Freedom-loving and cool on the outside, underneath they need a partner to cuddle up to. They're more focused than most Aquarians on creating financial security for themselves and loved ones. They enjoy cooking and all the sensual pleasures, but they will still have a need for personal freedom now and then. They might walk out one day for no other reason than to prove they can. They always come back, though, because both signs are fixed; they don't like change once they are settled. They are a difficult person to understand because they are both stable and unreliable.

AQUARIUS SUN/GEMINI MOON

These two air signs combined create someone who is a thinker. They're verbally clever and likely to shock. Words are their be-all and end-all, so they would make a great off-the-wall comedian or writer. They're a fabulous speaker because they are hilarious and close to the mark. However, they're not a great partner; they need movement, conversation, and freedom in every aspect of their lives. Mates will need to be earthy and practical, because they certainly aren't.

AQUARIUS SUN/CANCER MOON

Cancer adds an emotional element to the usually cool, detached manner of Aquarius, so this person needs emotional stability and a family base to work from. Therefore, they will settle down and commit, but the desire for freedom will waft across them now and then, causing them to disappear for a day or two. Ideally, their job will take them away, giving them room to breathe. They're compassionate underneath but cool on the surface, so this is an unusual combination. They're not practical, but they're very caring.

AQUARIUS SUN/LEO MOON

This person is a real rebel who wants to live a larger-than-average life. They seek the limelight and, because of their Aquarian wackiness, they are an unusual, unpredictable, and funny character who loves being on show. They will always need to be the centre of attention and adore any praise that comes their way. Warm and loving, they will choose unusual partners who stand out from the crowd as much as they do. Even if they're partnered, there will always be something slightly aloof about them—they rarely give their entire heart to anyone. They just want to stand in the spotlight and be applauded!

AQUARIUS SUN/VIRGO MOON

This is a more shy, modest, and retiring Aquarian with an inner sense of duty and responsibility. They worry about things. They can get a bit nitpicky and critical when stressed, but they're wonderfully calm and cool on the surface, with an open door for friends and neighbours. However, they always keep a bit of themselves back, so they never feel totally committed. Aquarius might suddenly walk out and leave their responsibilities behind, but they will always return because of their sense of duty. They're good at technical subjects that require an eye for detail.

AQUARIUS SUN/LIBRA MOON

This is a very cool, elegant, calm, logical, and balanced person who will have a touch of the unusual about them. They're clever and cerebral, able to appreciate every point of view, so they rarely get ruffled. Libra hates unpleasant, aggressive, rude people, so this combination is more judgmental than most Aquarius suns. They're not practical or warm, but nevertheless, they will want a partner. Ideally, they will live in a nicer-than-average house and neighbourhood. They have an eye for design, but they'll want it to have a quirky twist. Partners will need to be earthy and practical because they aren't. They might live beyond their means.

AQUARIUS SUN/SCORPIO MOON

This person is very cool and detached on the surface, but dig a bit deeper and passions boil. They need a one-on-one intense relationship, yet they are personally aloof at times. They may appear unconcerned, but they are actually watching all the time. Actions will be unpredictable—sometimes unkind—when they feel betrayed or hurt. They are very obstinate, controlling, and fixed in their views and ways; they will never change because they are who they are, so take it or leave it. A strong partner is required.

AQUARIUS SUN/SAGITTARIUS MOON

This is a real wild child who will never be tamed or tied down. They seek a life of freedom and excitement that is slightly different from others'. Totally unpredictable and sometimes impulsive, they will have hundreds of friends from all walks of life. They're unlikely to want a long-term commitment, but they might hang around if partners take all the strain and allow them to wander free. They're inclined to be shockingly blunt, and they will always laugh at their own jokes.

AQUARIUS SUN/CAPRICORN MOON

This person will appear unconventional, but underneath they are driven to make money and build a family line based on traditional values. With that being said, they will find unusual ways of doing so. Ideally, their partner will attend to the household and children because they will be working long hours, often when the spirit of genius moves them. Knowing Aquarius, that could be in the middle of the night. They will make it big, but via an unpredictable path. When they do break free from work, they love spending time with friends. It would be best if their partner was both active and sociable.

AQUARIUS SUN/PISCES MOON

This is a very otherworldly person who is not at all realistic. They're very cool and detached yet receptive and understanding; they will listen to others' problems but not be of any practical help. They see the larger picture and wonder why people get themselves into so many complicated messes. They're probably artistic, but in an unconventional way, as Aquarius loves to surprise and shock; they tend to be at the forefront of new movements in art and music. They're not at all practical, so partners will need to be supportive and capable. Overall, this is a very sweet, kind, cool person who will live life in an unusual way. Commune living would suit them as long as they could go their own way.

PISCES SUN/MOON COMBINATIONS

Pisces is a water sign, a gentle, kind soul with deep compassion, so the last thing they need is a water moon, because it swamps them with even more empathy and does little to help them manage the real world. An earth moon would be beneficial, as it provides common sense and grounds them. Air moons work too, as they bestow logic, and fire moons supply much-needed drive and energy.

PISCES SUN/ARIES MOON

An impulsive drive pushes this person forward into situations that end up making them uneasy. Warmer than most Pisceans, they will still need independence and solitude. Sometimes they will be on track; sometimes they will be wobbling all over the place. They take on activities with enthusiasm and then realise they are overfaced; it's the same with people. Kind and friendly, they are always willing to help, but they have limited energy levels. They're guided by their intuition. They are very intuitive (possibly psychic), but so totally trusting they tend to ignore their own inner warnings which means they often get hurt. They need a grounded partner to anchor them, but one who allows them to make their own mistakes.

PISCES SUN/TAURUS MOON

This is a sweet, gentle person who needs stability and security in their emotional life. They're more placid and cuddly than most Pisceans. They're keen to make financial gains so they can relax and feel safe. They give the impression of being reliable, but they're inclined to disappear now and then so they can be alone. They will extend themselves to create a homely atmosphere, but they find it hard to maintain their momentum. It's important they have someone they can cuddle up to who makes them feel safe.

PISCES SUN/GEMINI MOON

This is a very restless person who is logical one minute and fuzzy the next. They are very sociable and chatty—inclined to talk too much, actually—and will develop lots of interests and hobbies throughout their lives. Cool and unpredictable, it is impossible to tie them down to a time or place. They're prone to slipping away when others try to catch them, so they will find committed relationships to be a challenge. They're very complex, imaginative, and clever with words.

PISCES SUN/CANCER MOON

This is a deeply emotional and caring person who will go the extra mile to help mankind. They must live a life that makes a difference. They give it their all, but they have a limited amount of energy and stamina and need downtime to recover. There is no end to suffering, so despite doing what they can, it never seems like enough. Extra sensitive, they pick up all sorts of messages and vibrations. Because of this, they are easily hurt, but they're always forgiving.

They need emotional security, so they will want a home and family—however, they will struggle with the practical demands. Partners will need to be their rock.

PISCES SUN/LEO MOON

Leo always likes to be the centre of attention, so they will seek the limelight and recognition, perhaps for their artistic or musical endeavours. But it takes all of their energy to be showy, as Pisces is quite shy and likes to retreat. They can be extravagant. They enjoy dressing up and going to nice places, and with their charm, they manage to get others running around after them. After they've been in the limelight, they will need time to recover and restore their inner calm. They have an inner warmth but appear quite cool and impersonal. At the very least, they need to be important to their family, the hub around which all revolves. This person is kind, sweet, understanding, and gentle—as long as people do their bidding. They can ignore the mundane aspects of life quite easily!

PISCES SUN/VIRGO MOON

Easily agitated and prone to criticism when tired or upset, this combination is also very kind and dutiful. They are more practical than most Pisceans, but they're prone to worrying and fretting, so they may lose the plot. They often find themselves overwhelmed by the details they see so clearly, yet lack the stamina to deal with. They suffer from a restless spirit, yet they experience guilt whenever they try to escape to somewhere calm. A grounded, placid earth sign will be a haven, an anchor, for them.

PISCES SUN/LIBRA MOON

This is an incredibly sweet, cool, calm, and attractive person with the kindest personality, but they will need to be sheltered from life because they cannot cope with aggression, negative people, or challenging situations. They will appear serene and in control, but they are always trying to balance their logical nature with their emotionally receptive side. In principle, Pisces is psychic, but Libra believes in logic, so it's hard for this person to handle both aspects. They will look for a wealthy partner who can protect them.

PISCES SUN/SCORPIO MOON

Two water signs together will create a deeply emotional and receptive person, open to nuances and vibrations, who is both forgiving and yet unable to let go of past hurts. Incredibly sensitive, they always have an eye on being used, so it is hard for them to believe others aren't out to hurt them. This can result in paranoia, so they need a grounded, earthy, sexy mate who can bring a bit of common sense to their emotionally turbulent feelings. They make intense yet hard to fathom partners; it's likely they won't even understand themselves!

PISCES SUN/SAGITTARIUS MOON

This is a very restless person who is forever doing things, then leaving them half-finished to do something else. They rely on intuition in life and are prone to dashing off on a wild goose chase. They're not at all logical or grounded. In fact, they're very hard to pin down; they slip away all the time. This is because they need to feel free and unfettered to follow their inner voice. They're not interested in financial, emotional, or material security because they have an innate feeling that the universe will provide all they need. Because of this, they will be unrealistic and live beyond their means, so a mate who provides for them would be ideal.

PISCES SUN/CAPRICORN MOON

Hardworking and kind, this person tends to worry and grapples with low self-esteem, so they need a home and family to anchor them. Quite traditional, everything they do will be for their loved ones. They have grand dreams, but they don't always have the wherewithal to implement them. They're capable of marrying for money so they can have security and then be free to follow their own tune, which might be artistic. Whatever their passion is, they would ideally like to make money from it and be recognised as a force in their field. A fire sign partner will add some excitement and energy to their life.

PISCES SUN/AQUARIUS MOON

This is a very off-the-wall oddball who lives life to their own tune, which will be totally out of step with everyone else's. Gentle, kind, cool, and detached, they have a unique and original personality and would never presume to tell anyone else how to live. Accepting and nonjudgmental, they live and let live. They are an escapist with a need for personal freedom, so it's questionable if they will want a life partner, but if they do, someone practical and earthy might be wise. If they are creative—and it's likely—their output will be imaginative and visionary.

PISCES SUN/PISCES MOON

This person is a dreamer. They're imaginative and psychic, yet they appear hopelessly fuzzy and disorganised. Somehow, they manage to muddle through life. They're extremely receptive, understanding, sympathetic, and supportive, but they're also timid. They have little energy for ongoing situations. They are not equipped for today's busy, ambitious, materialistic world, so they will need a gatekeeping partner to handle things and protect them from becoming overfaced, which may happen frequently. There is an overriding need for space and calm, and this combination will heighten their psychic/artistic rendencies.

CONCLUSION

Understanding your sun, moon, and rising signs and the way they influence how you act is the first step in discovering the real you.

If you've enjoyed reading this book, why not study astrology in more depth? My book *Birth Chart Interpretation Plain & Simple* makes understanding your whole birth chart easy. It leads you gently through all aspects of your chart with explanations every step of the way, and it is specifically designed for those with no, or very little, prior knowledge of astrology. The sun, moon, and rising sign are just the tip of the iceburg—there is so much more just waiting to be discovered!

TO WRITE TO THE AUTHOR

If you wish to contact the author or would like more information about this book, please write to the author in care of Llewellyn Worldwide Ltd. and we will forward your request. Both the author and publisher appreciate hearing from you and learning of your enjoyment of this book and how it has helped you. Llewellyn Worldwide Ltd. cannot guarantee that every letter written to the author can be answered, but all will be forwarded. Please write to:

Andrea Taylor
℅ Llewellyn Worldwide
2143 Wooddale Drive
Woodbury, MN 55125-2989

Please enclose a self-addressed stamped envelope for reply, or $1.00 to cover costs. If outside the U.S.A., enclose an international postal reply coupon.

Many of Llewellyn's authors have websites with additional information and resources. For more information, please visit our website at http://www.llewellyn.com.